AF600560

THE CATHOLIC UNIVERSITY OF AMERICA
CANON LAW STUDIES
NUMBER 91

CANONICAL ANTE-NUPTIAL PROMISES AND THE CIVIL LAW

AN HISTORICAL SYNOPSIS AND COMMENTARY

A DISSERTATION

SUBMITTED TO THE FACULTY OF CANON LAW OF THE CATHOLIC UNIVERSITY OF AMERICA IN PARTIAL FULFILLMENT OF THE REQUIREMENT FOR THE DEGREE OF DOCTOR OF CANON LAW

BY
REV. ROBERT J. WHITE, A.B., LL.B., S.T.B., J.C.L.

THE CATHOLIC UNIVERSITY OF AMERICA
WASHINGTON, D. C.
1934

Nihil Obstat:

JOSEPHUS E. McCARTHY, D.D.,
Episcopus Portlandensis.

Portlandensis, die XXI Maii, 1934.

PRINTED BY
THE DOLPHIN PRESS
PHILADELPHIA, PA.

FOREWORD

THE recent decree of the Holy See in reference to ante-nuptial promises in mixed marriages attracted great public interest to this important question. In order to understand the present legislation, it is necessary to examine again the history of the position of the Church in regard to these marriages. The reference in the decree to the attitude of the civil authority in respect of the fulfillment of these ante-nuptial promises makes it imperative to probe critically into the existing decisions of our civil law.

This study seeks to analyze the court decisions in the English-speaking countries of the world and particularly the decisions of the English and the American courts.

The writer wishes to express his thanks to the faculty of the School of Canon Law of the Catholic University of America and to His Excellency, Philip Bernardini, former Dean of the School, for generous assistance in the preparation of this work. He also wishes to acknowledge his appreciation of the assistance of John McD. Fox, Dean of the School of Law, Catholic University of America, the Rev. Dr. Patrick Dignan, Hon. John J. Burns and Dr. Frederick DeSlovere.

R. J. W.

TABLE OF CONTENTS

CHAPTER I

INTRODUCTION

THE recent decree on ante-nuptial promises in mixed marriages issued by the Holy Office [1] has again brought into prominence the mind of the Church upon this important question. The particular reasons for its issue, and the applicability of its far-reaching provisions, particularly those rendering void any dispensation granted contrary to its mandates, have led to a new interest in the whole subject among scholars, the press, and the people in general.[2] In the popular use of the broad term "mixed marriages", one must not lose sight of the drastic distinction in Canon Law between "mixed religion" and "disparity of cult".[3] For the former applies properly only to marriages between a Catholic and a baptized non-Catholic whether heretic or schismatic, while the latter applies properly only to those marriages between Catholics and infidels, unbaptized persons.[4] The impediment of mixed religion is a legal

[1] *Acta Apostolicae Sedis*, XXIV (1932), 15; *infra*, p. 40.

[2] The press in a hasty and uncritical appraisal has made unfounded conclusions which require refutation and a re-statement of the legal implications of the so-called promises in these marriages. For a typical press statement see *New York Times*, Feb. 6, 1932, p. 15.

"After this decree, both parties will know that if their promises are not accompanied by a firm intention to fulfill them, the dispensation will become null and void. . . . This will suffice to persuade them that their union is not legitimate matrimony but only concubinage."

For the reply see, Dr. V. Schaaf, *New York Times*, Feb. 14, II, 20:6.

For current periodical references, see, *Christian Century*, April 6, 1932, 436; *Christian Century*, April 27, 1932, 547; *Irish Eccl. Record* (May, 1932), Vol. 39, 532 ff.; *Catholic World* (March, 1932), Vol. 134, 745; Rev. Valentine Schaaf, *Am. Eccl. Review* (April, 1932), Vol. 86, p. 408 ff.

[3] Code of Canon Law, Canons 1036, 1060-64, 1070, 1071.

[4] P. Gasparri, *De Matrimonio*, editio nova ad mentem Codicis I. C. (Rome, Typis Polyglottis Vaticanis, 1932), n. 438.

prohibition which renders such a marriage illicit but not invalid in the absence of a dispensation;[5] in contrast, the impediment of disparity of cult renders such a marriage without a dispensation not only illicit but wholly null and void.[6] However the provisions of the required ante-nuptial promises in both types of marriage are the same.[7] Any critical inquiry into the canonical treatment of the problem of mixed marriages, in the broad sense of all marriages of Catholics with non-Catholics, must proceed *pari passu* with an inquiry into the particular historical background that gave rise to the various writings and decrees of Popes and Councils. Care should be taken not to attempt to read more into texts than they justify and historical gaps are better left unfilled than bridged by conjecture.

The early Christian church struggling at first on the shores of Asia Minor was profoundly influenced by the survival of some of the Jewish customs and prohibitions of the Old Testament.[8] The Hebrews had been enjoined from marrying pagans.[9] While it has been said that this injunction passed over with binding force upon all in the Christian dispensation,[10] it may be seriously questioned if such a reason states accurately the basis for the development of the doctrine of these impediments in the new dispensation.[11] Christianity faced its struggle

[5] Canon 1036; Gasparri, *De Matrimonio*, n. 439; H. A. Ayrinhac, *Marriage Legislation in the New Code of Canon Law*, new, revised ed. (New York, Benziger Bros., 1932), pp. 52 ff., 98 ff.

[6] Canon 1036, § 2, Canon 1070; Gasparri, *De Matrimonio*, n. 567; Ayrinhac, *Marriage Legislation*, p. 136 ff.

[7] Canons 1060-64, 1071; see decree, *infra*, p. ——.

[8] Acts X, 14; XV, 5-22; XXI, 20-26; Prat, *The Theology of St. Paul* (London, Burns, Oates and Washburn, 1926), I, 17 ff., 44 ff., 50 ff., 202; II, 36, 223.

[9] Deut., VII, 2-4; Exodus, XXXIV, 15, 16; Roskovany, *De Matrimoniis Mixtis* (Pestini, G. Emich, 1042), IV, p. II.

[10] Bellarmine, *De Sacram. Matr.*, cap. XXIII, Op. Omnia, III, 835 (Neapoli, C. P. Lauriel, 1872).

[11] Prat, *op. cit.*, II, 223 ff.; Esmein, *Le Mariage en Droit Canonique*, II, 336.

for existence against " the orbis-terrarum—the Graeco-Roman world ",[12] in which " nearly all earthly power was held by the City of Rome . . . from the Atlantic to the Euphrates, from the Rhine and the Danube to the Cataracts of the Nile ".[13] " It was a closely knit, well-compacted union of peoples with one mind, common aspirations and a common culture[14]. . . There was a universal understanding of the two leading languages, Latin and Greek, common law and common interests[15] . . . The state enjoyed full jurisdiction over the lives and possessions of its citizens and regulated marriage. . . ."[16] Though Christianity and heathenism were to engage in a death struggle, yet Christianity was to gain its converts from people solidly grounded in Roman tradition and Roman law. And for our understanding of the problem of mixed marriage in the early Church and expressions used in the regulations as found in the Fathers and Church councils—a brief consideration of the Roman law in respect to marriage impediments seems helpful. The Roman Law recognized legal obstacles to marriage in foreign citizenship, slavery, blood relationship within prohibited degrees and other disabilities.[17] These obstacles rendered the marriages in violation of such prohibitions invalid.[18]

Moreover the Canon Law was influenced profoundly by the Roman Law concept of the *paterfamilias*. His power over the *filiifamilias*, so extreme in the early law as to be characterized

[12] Shahan, *The Beginnings of Christianity* (New York, Benziger Bros., 1903), p. 11.

[13] Shahan, *op. cit.*, p. 12.

[14] P. J. Healy, *The Valerian Persecution* (Boston, Houghton Mifflin & Co., 1905), p. 5.

[15] Healy, *op. cit.*, p. 5.

[16] Healy, *op. cit.*, p. 15.

[17] Corbett, *The Roman Law of Marriage* (Oxford, Clarendon Press, 1930), p. 24.

[18] Corbett, *op. cit.*, p. 34 ff.; C. P. Sherman, *Roman Law in the Modern World* (Boston, Boston Book Co., 1917), p. 47 ff.

by the expression *ius vitae necisque* [19] had indeed declined to a great extent. But his control persisted in respect to the choice of the *filiifamilias* of a marriage partner. And his consent was necessary for the validity of such a marriage.[20] This enables one to appreciate more clearly the strong injunctions of early councils such as Elvira directed to the parents forbidding them to allow their children, particularly the daughters to marry pagans or Jews.[21] The later Roman Law, though not using the term impediment, expressly forbade the marriage of Christians with Jews.[22] And such legislation becoming incorporated in particular councils, was in turn adopted by the Visigoths [23] and Franks [24] and is found persisting in modern legislation.[25]

An examination of the early fathers reveals fewer instances of direct reference to mixed marriage than one would naturally expect.[26] This may be explained however by the *a fortiori* argument in the repeated injunctions against even social intercourse with schismatics, heretics and infidels which would render marriage with such persons unthinkable.[27] The jurisdiction of the church over marriage is attested in the very early epistle written by St. Ignatius to Polycarp (110) in the words " it becomes both men and women to form their union with the approval of the bishop that their marriage may be according to

[19] J. V. Sangmeister, *Force and Fear* (Washington, Catholic University of America, 1932), p. 24 ff.

[20] Corbett, *op. cit.*, pp. 57, 58, 60.

[21] Canon 16—Mansi, II, 8.

[22] Code Theod. III, 7, 2; Code Theod. IX, 7, 5; Code Theod. XVI, 8, 6; Code I, 9, 6 (A 388).

[23] Esmein, *Le Mariage en Droit Canonique*, p. 11.

[24] Esmein, *op. cit.*, p. 14.

[25] Austrian Civil Code, 64; see Sherman, *op. cit.*, 48.

[26] Roskovany, *De Matrimoniis Mixtis*, Vols. III, IV which contain early *monumenta*.

[27] H. J. Feije, *De Matrimoniis Mixtis*, p. 65 ff.; Esmein, *Le Mariage en Droit Canonique*, I, 5; C. F. Esmein, *op. cit.*, II, 216 ff.

the Lord and not after their own lust ".[28] Tertullian writing in Africa in the second century inveighed against the marriage of Christians with pagans and interpreted the injunction of St. Paul to marry " only in the Lord " not in the sense of a persuasive counsel but as an authoritative command.[29] Such marriages, he said, were fraught with dangers of loss of faith, a lack of appreciation of the true nature of marriage and even idolatry.[30] St. Cyprian,[31] also of Carthage, writing in the same century, and St. Augustine later, warned Christians against such marriages [32] and reminded them of the historical examples of the Old Testament.[32a] St. Ambrose,[33] St. Jerome [34] and St. Zeno [35] in Italy, decried such marriages in a vigorous tone and the first cited Holy Scripture, stressing the sacramental nature of marriage and the vital difference between baptized and pagan.[36]

The scriptural prohibition, the strong injunctions of St. Paul, the Roman Law provisions, and the vigorous attacks upon mixed marriages by these early Church authorities crystalized in the enactments of early particular and general

[28] Ante-Nicene Fathers, I, 95, vol. 2, C V.

[29] " De Nubendo vero in Domino, cum dicit tantum in Domino, iam non suadet, sed exerte iubet." *Ad Uxorem*, Lib. II, cap. 1—M. P. L., I, 1292-1293; J. Köhne, *Die Ehen Zwischen Christen und Heiden in den Ersten Christlichen Jahrhunderten* (Paderborn, Bonifacius-Druckerei, 1931), p. 1 ff.

[30] *Adversus Marcion*, Lib. V. Cap. 7—M. P. L., II, 487; *Liber De Corona*, cap. 13—M. P. L., II, 96.

[31] *De Lapsis*, cap. 6— *Corp. Scr. Eccl. Lat.*, Vol. III, par. I, 240.

[32] *Epist.*, XXIII, n. 5—M. P. L., XXXIII, 97.

[32a] *Ad. Quirinium*, Lib. III, cap. 62—*Corp. Scr. Eccl. Lat.*, Vol. II, par. I, p. 166.

[33] *Epist. 19, Ad Vigilium*—M. P. L., XVI, 984-985.

[34] *Adversus Jovinianum*, Lib. I, n. 10—M. P. L., XXIII, 225.

[35] Tractatus, Lib. I, Tract. V, nn. 7-9, M. P. L., XI, 307-311; Köhne, *op. cit.*, p. 63 ff.

[36] *De Abraham*, Lib. I, cap. 9, n. 84, M. P. L., XIV, 451; *Expositio in Ps.*, CXVIII, Sermo 20, n. 48—M. P. L., XV, 1499; *Expositio Evang.*, sec. Lucam, Lib. VIII, n. 2, M. P. L., XV, 1765.

councils.[37] The Council of Elvira (306) enacted the earliest conciliar legislation forbidding marriage with non-Christians. Although the legislation also included prohibitions again marriages with pagans and heretics, the canons were particularly drastic in their provisions against marriages with Jews.[38] The legislation of the Spanish Council was enacted by the later French Council of Arles (314).[39] The Eastern Councils of Laodicea (343, 381) forbade parents giving their children in marriage to heretics.[40] In Africa, the Councils of Hippo (393),[41] and Carthage (397, 436)[42] enjoined clerics from giving their children in mixed marriages. And this evil was also attacked in the ecumenical Council of Chalcedon (451).[43] While these early fathers and legislators in Church councils had affirmatively pointed out in many writings and canons the existence of Church prohibitions against marriages with non-Christians, they had used words and contexts interchangeably in referring to disparity of cult and mixed religion. Thus it is impossible to establish from them the existence of a well-defined distinction between the impediment of disparity of cult and that of mixed religion.[44] Most authorities agree that the distinction became defined as a growth of custom which finally became universal rather than by any single universal pronouncement by Church authority or particular enactment by a council. As to the date when this custom became universal, the authors disagree, fixing the time all the way from the sixth to the thirteenth century but favoring for the most part the twelfth century. The nineteenth canon of the Second Council of

[37] Roskovany, *De Matrimoniis Mixtis,* Vol. IV, p. iv.

[38] Canons 16, 17, 50, 58—Mansi, II, 8.

[39] Canon 11—Mansi, II, 472.

[40] Canon 10—Mansi II, 565; Canon 31—Mansii II, 569.

[41] Canon 12—Mansi III, 921.

[42] Canon 12—Mansi III, 882; Canon 70—Mansi III, 957.

[43] Mansi, VII, 388.

[44] Gasparri, *De Matrimonio,* II, 258.

Orleans (533) marks the first particular legislation which defined the existence of disparity of cult in marriages between Christians and Jews as a separate, distinct and diriment impediment.[45] The spirit of the drastic provisions of the second council of Orleans against marriages with Jews may be traced through the later French,[46] Spanish [47] and Italian [48] Councils. From an examination of these, it is evident that the earliest development of the diriment impediment was that which existed in marriages of Christians with Jews, and apparently the impediment in marriages with infidels was deemed in the same category as those with schismatics and heretics and thus considered as only a prohibitive rather than as in later times a diriment impediment.

Gratian prefaced a passage from St. Ambrose with the dictum that in marriages of the faithful with infidels, making no distinction, they must be separated ("separandi sunt").[49] If, as some assert, this term included all who were not Catholics, it represented a new attitude which can be explained only by the acute religious feeling of that time. The exact nature of the impediment in marriages of Catholics with schismatics and heretics was to be given much more critical attention when in the following centuries the Church was assailed by several heresies, which spread widely in territory and gained many zealous adherents. The religious ardor of the Crusaders, the Inquisitions, and the campaigns against encroaching enemies had real effects in the intensive analysis of the nature of these impediments. Pope Innocent III in the twelfth century is credited with the first explanation of the merely prohibitive

[45] Mansi, VIII, 838.

[46] Council of Aubergne (535), Canon 6—Mansi, VIII, 861; Fourth Council of Orleans (541), Canon 31—Mansi, IX, 118; Council of Meaux (845), Canon 73—Mansi, XIV, 836-839.

[47] Third Council of Toledo (589), Canon 14—Mansi, IX, 996; Fourth Council of Toledo (663), Canon 63—Mansi, X, 634.

[48] First Council of Rome (743), Canon 10—Mansi, XII, 374.

[49] C. 15, C. XXVIII, q. 1—*De Abraham*, Lib. I, cap. 9, no. 84.

character of the impediment of mixed religion basing it upon the nature of marriage as affected by the sacrament of baptism.[50] He reasoned that the sacrament of faith might be the foundation of a *matrimonium ratum* between two baptized persons though not members of the same religious faith, as Catholic and schismatic or heretic. Hence such a marriage would be valid though illicit. In the absence of baptism as a foundation for marriage,—as in the union of a Catholic with a Jew or infidel,—the marriage would lack validity and hence be null as well as illicit. This explanation found favor in the great theological writings of the following century.[51] And Pope Innocent IV although prescribing drastic punishments for those Catholics who married heretics nevertheless seemed also to admit the validity of such unions.[52] And this opinion seems confirmed as well in the decree of the Council of Pressburg (309).[53]

The profound world-wide changes of the following centuries influenced powerfully the history of the mixed marriage problem. The sixteenth century witnessed a tremendous religious upheaval, extensive new territorial discoveries and great missionary efforts in both the Orient and in the West. This marked the definite beginning of a new era[54] lasting to our own day when the problem of mixed marriage became of vital importance and increasingly more difficult to control.[55] The difficulties of preserving its membership in the face of the threatening losses owing to great heretical movements in some parts of the world and of spreading its divine mission in the face of overwhelming odds in the newly discovered parts

[50] C. 7, X, *de divortiis*, IV, 19.

[51] Summa Theol. IIIa suppl. q. 59, Art. I, ad. 5.

[52] C. 14, *de haereticis*, V, 2, in VI; Feije, *op. cit.*, p. 8.

[53] Canon 8—Mansi, XXV, 222.

[54] F. X. Funk, *History of the Church* (London, Burns and Oates, 1914), Vol. II, p. 158 ff.

[55] Esmein, *Le Mariage en Droit Canonique*, I, 31 ff.

sorely tried the patience, wisdom, and prudence of the Church. Ever faithful to her duty to safe-guard the sacrament of marriage, the Church attempted by all possible means to prevent her children from entering marriages with non-Catholics. Failing to deter them in the face of impossible odds, she did her utmost to provide safe-guards for the divine faith as preliminary necessary conditions for the granting of a dispensation to a Catholic to marry a schismatic, heretic, infidel or Jew. The Council of Trent did not enact legislation directly upon marriages with non-Catholics.[56] But the decree "*Tametsi*" excluded the possibility of such marriages indirectly because it required the celebration of the marriage before the *parochus proprius* for validity, and forbade pastors to perform mixed marriages without a Papal dispensation or an abjuration of heresy.[57] This however was ineffective in controlling the evil because it soon became evident that different localities assumed different practices, discipline and customs, and in some localities, it seems that mixed marriages were tolerated without restriction.[58]

The situation became further complicated by the fact that ruling sovereigns of several countries including England, France, Spain and Bavaria became parties to petitions for dispensations acting for themselves personally or for their children. This involved consequences far more serious than the personal and immediate issue involved, for the religion of the ruling power became often an important and controlling influence in the religious profession and practice of many of its subjects.[59] An early example of such a petition was that of Henry, of Bavaria, in 1604 during the reign of Pope Clement VIII.[60]

[56] Roskovany, *De Matrimoniis Mixtis*, I, 7.

[57] Conc. Trident., sess. XXIV, *de reformo matr.*, cap. 1—Mansi, XXXIII, 152-153.

[58] Feije, *op. cit.*, pp. 14, 18, 121 ff.

[59] Funk, *op. cit.*, II, 99, 110 ff.

[60] Albitius, *De Inconstantia in Fide*, Cap. XXXVI, n. 206.

During the following hundred and fifty years, Papal dispensations in mixed marriages were restricted to those cases which had the nature of a *causa publica* because affecting members of the nobility. Often these dispensations were made the subject matter of long and involved diplomatic agreements. They contained such safeguards,—required as conditions for the celebration of these marriages,—as early promise of conversion, the abjuration of heresy, the provision relative to future custody of the children of the marriage, the freedom of the exercise of religion on the part of the Catholic, and the many complicated collateral promises. And since these cases were regarded as *gravis publica,* the particular written promises required in each individual case differed according to the conditions peculiar to the situation demanding such dispensation. These were the forerunners of the formal *cautiones* of to-day. The widespread and far-reaching effects of the Reformation in England, Germany, and Poland, the devastating influence of the French Revolution, and the many problems of advancing missionary efforts in strange lands—all contributed in rendering acute the distressing problem of mixed marriages. Unwillingly, the Holy See mitigated her discipline to some extent and granted dispensations, and later allowed some bishops to grant a limited number of dispensations in such marriages.

Dispensations were now no longer restricted to cases of nobility as affected by a *causa publica* but could also be granted to others if affected with a *causa gravis.* What facts may constitute a *gravis causa* have been enumerated in a list of sixteen causes given by the Sacred Congregation of the Propaganda.[61] While many canonists differ as to a complete list, all seem to agree upon certain facts as constituting a justifiable claim for dispensation. Prominent among these are: the predominance of infidels, heretics or schismatics in a particular region; the avoidance of scandal; danger of apostasy

[61] Tanquerey, *Synopsis Theologiae Moralis* (Paris, Desclee 1925), T I. Sect. 1065, p. 625.

or marriage before a civil or non-Catholic minister if the dispensation is denied; and a well-founded hope of conversion of the non-Catholic party.[62] Other cases singly or in combination could also constitute such *gravis causa.*

Just as the earlier dispensations to the nobility were the forerunners of the later dispensations to the common people, so the formal promises, exacted of the nobles, became to some extent the models of the later *cautiones* in the ordinary case, particularly in the provisions affecting the rearing of the offspring in the Catholic religion. The exigencies of the difficult conditions encountered in missionary countries may explain the absence of any absolute requirement in the faculties given to the missionaries demanding the formal *cautiones* as a condition to the granting of a dispensation. However, due precautions were always required to insure the rearing of the children of such mixed marriages in the Catholic faith. This was often satisfied in missionary countries in those cases in which the father was of the Catholic faith, for according to the law and customs prevalent in many countries, he controlled the religious education of the child. In 1782, Pope Pius VI in an answer to the Cardinal Archbishop of Malines prescribed the following conditions among others for the licit assistance of the parish priest as an informal or material witness in Belgian marriages where the Civil Law coerced the assistance of pastors at mixed marriages. The heretic must give a formal declaration in writing, sealed with an oath and signed conjointly with two witnesses that the Catholic be left the free exercise of the Catholic religion, and that all the children regardless of sex, be educated in the Catholic faith. The Catholic was likewise to give a sworn, written, and witnessed declaration foreswearing all apostasy, promising to educate all the

[62] Gasparri, *De Matrimonio,* I, Sect. 448, p. 264; Ayrinhac, *Marriage Legislation,* 103; Capello, *De Sacramentis,* III, 360; Petrovits, *New Church Law on Matrimony* (Washington, Catholic University of America, 1919), 184.

children in the Catholic faith, and to employ effective means to procure the conversion of the non-Catholic spouse.[63]

From this time the constant practice of the church required formal promises whether the dispensation was granted by the Holy See, as had been the custom, or granted by the Bishops, who towards the end of the eighteenth century were given a fixed number of dispensations to be granted in a certain given period. Pope Pius VI had thus decreed as a condition for the granting of a dispensation not only the promise to educate all of the children in the Catholic faith, but also the promise on the part of the non-Catholic to permit the Catholic party freedom in the exercise of religious duties. After the date of this rescript (1782), these *cautiones* were strictly required as attested by many other rescripts, decrees and encyclicals.[64] In explaining the reasoning of the requirement that these promises be given in mixed marriages, authentic statements of church officials and the opinions of some noted canonists rested the necessity upon the demands of divine law.[65]

[63] Rescript, ad Card. Archiep. Mechlinien., 13 Iul. 1782, n. 4—*Fontes,* n. 471, n. 4. *Secundo,* ut exigat et recipiat a contrahente haeretico *declarationem in scriptis,* qua cum *iuramento,* praesentibus duobus testibus, qui debebunt et ipsi subscribere, *obliget se ad permittendum comparti usum liberum religionis catholicae et ad educandum in eadem omnes liberos nascituros sine ulla sexus distinctione*; . . .

Tertio, ut et ipse contrahens catholicus declarationem edat a se et duobus testibus subscriptam, in qua cum iuramento promittat, non tantum se nunquam apostataturum a religione sua catholica, sed educaturum in ipsa omnem prolem nascituram, et procuraturum se efficaciter conversionem alterius contrahentis acatholici.

[64] See decrees and authorities treated in notes 65 to 87 inclusive. S. C. S. Off. (Quebec), 10 Sept. 1920—*Fontes,* n. 859; instr. (ad Archiep. Quebecen.), 16 Sept. 1824—*Fontes,* n. 866; (ad Archiep. Corcyren.), 3 Ian. 1871—*Fontes,* n. 1013; litt. (S. Germani), 17 Feb. 1875—*Fontes,* n. 1039; (ad Ep. Aurelianen.), 6 Iun. 1879—*Fontes,* n. 1064; instr. (ad omnes Ep. Ritus Orient.), 12 Dec. 1888—*Fontes,* n. 1112.

[65] See authorities cited, Schenk, *op. cit.,* n. 44, p. 60; see, Ter Haar, *De Matrimoniis Mixtis Eorumque Remediis* (Turin-Marietti, 1931), p. 55 ff.; Ayrinhac, *op. cit.,* 105; Augustine, *Commentary on Canon Law* (Herder, St. Louis, 1920), 5, 148; Wernz-Vidal, *Ius Matrimoniale,* sect. 177, p. 190; C. G. Gasparri, *op. cit.,* I, sect. 450, p. 265.

As to the further requirement that the promises be reduced to formal writings, this seemed to rest upon the advisability of obtaining solemn covenants which would impress the parties more deeply and be available as evidence in the event of attempted repudiation.

In the confusion of the various customs of different nationalities and sectional traditions, the Church determined to bring about as nearly as possible a uniform discipline as to the granting of dispensations, and in particular to insist upon the requirement of the *cautiones*. The struggle was to be long and bitter, and the missionary progress, favorable in one territory was to be offset by governmental influence and wavering ecclesiastical authorities in others. It must be borne in mind that the Church, although possessing universal authority, faced the different established customs of many nationalities. In many places the custom had secured a foothold of entering mixed marriages without even obtaining a dispensation. The tolerance of the Church in refraining from declaring invalid mixed marriages in which the *cautiones* had not been given, can be understood more easily if we keep in mind the struggle of the Church against the greater evil of this growing custom of mixed marriages without the obtaining of a dispensation of any kind. In addition, peculiar local difficulties arose from drastic anti-Catholic laws and regulations.

The German bishops had allowed the practice of neglecting to obtain dispensations in mixed marriages to flourish. And thus provoked, several Pontiffs, particularly Benedict XIV,[66] Pius VIII[67] and Gregory XVI,[68] issued severe condemnation against such a custom. In Bavaria, the false notion that a mixed marriage could be contracted without a dispensation gained such a foothold that Pope Gregory XVI reprobated the custom and also called attention to the necessity of the *cautiones*

[66] *Ep. Ad Tuas*, 8 Aug., 1748, § 6—*Fontes*, n. 389.

[67] *Litt. ap. Litteris altero*, 25 Mart., 1830—*Fontes*, n. 482.

[68] *Ep. encycl. Summo iugiter*, 27 Maii, 1832, §§ 2, 6—*Fontes*, n. 484.

in those exceptional cases of mixed marriages in which dispensations should be granted.[69] In Hungary, the evil provoked the same pontiff to send a communication to the bishops in the same tenor, rebuking the laxness of Catholics entering marriages with non-Catholics, and laying down the absolute requirement of the *cautiones* in cases in which dispensation should be granted.[70] In Freiburg, these and added evils, which seriously threatened the discipline of the clergy as well as the people, occasioned a strong letter from Gregory XVI (1839) [71] in which he called attention to his earlier declaration to the Bishop of Bavaria (1832).[72] A few years later, (1846) he again directed attention to the requirement of the *cautiones* and forbade the giving of a blessing upon a marriage contracted without a dispensation, if the *cautiones* should be refused.[73]

Embarrassed by the civil law of Belgium, which compelled the assistance of Catholic pastors at mixed marriages, Pope Pius VI had given unwilling consent to the presence of the pastor as an informal witness, but had explicitly required the signing of the promises in such marriages.[74] Russia likewise legislated in the matter, issuing a decree which required that mixed marriages be celebrated before a priest of the state church, and further, that all children born of such unions be reared in the state Church.[75] The hostility in Canada, in reference to the promises for the religious up-bringing of the children of mixed marriages, caused the Bishop of Ottawa to seek counsel at Rome. And in a rescript, the bishops were advised by the Holy See to insist upon the *cautiones* even in the presence

[69] *Ep. encycl. Summo Igitur*, 27 Maii, 1832—*Fontes*, n. 484.

[70] *Litt. ap. Quas Vestro*, 30 Apr., 1841—*Fontes*, n. 497.

[71] *Ep. Dolorem*, 30 Nov., 1839—*Fontes*, n. 493.

[72] See note 69, *supra*.

[73] *Ep. Non sine gravi*, 23 Maii, 1846—*Fontes*, n. 503.

[74] See note 63, *supra*.

[75] Roskovany, *Matrimoniis Mixtis*, IV, sect. 776-77, p. 153.

of such opposition by the civil war.[76] The animus of the civil authorities in England, and even in the United States, in the matter of the control of the religious up-bringing, resting in such ante-nuptial agreements, is apparent in many opinions which are tested more fully in a subsequent chapter.[77]

In addition to positive, hostile laws and antagonistic judicial treatment by the courts, the Church was beset, particularly in missionary fields and notably in the Far East, by firmly established opposition to the formal signing of the promises. The Church tolerated a relaxation of her demands, as evidenced in some of the faculties for granting dispensations given to the authorities in some missionary countries.[78]

In the face of all these difficulties, the Church persistently adhered to her firm determination to insist upon the signing of the *cautiones* as a condition precedent to the granting of a dispensation for the marriage of any Catholic with any non-Catholic. And she reiterated her position in the matter in a world-wide decree to the bishops, issued November 15, 1858.[79] But the antipathy of the civil power continued, rapidly appearing in the various forms of impeding laws and regulations.

In Germany, the situation was particularly aggravated and led to several serious crises in the relations between the local governments and the bishops and the Holy See. According to the common law of Prussia (1794), the boys born of a mixed marriage were to be reared in the religion of the father, the girls in the religion of the mother. By a decree of November 21, 1803, the religion of the father was made predominant, and controlled the religion in which the girls as well as the

[76] Rescript *ad Episcopum* Ottawa in Canada, S. C. S. Officii, 17 Apr., 1879 —Gasparri, *op. cit.*, I, 268.

[77] See, *infra*, p. 49 ff.

[78] G. Payen, *De Matrimonio in Missionibus ac potissimum in Sinis* (Zi-Za-Wei, Typographia T'ou-Sè-Wè, 1929), III, sect. 874, 151 ff., Casus 98-99; III, 673 ff.

[79] *Instr. Secret. Stat. iussu Pii PP.*, IX,—Coll., n. 1169.

boys should be reared. This decree, however, was actually enforced only in the eastern provinces. But in 1825, this hostile imperial decree was extended and made effective in the enlarged territory of the Rhineland and Westphalia, which included the dioceses of Cologne, Treves, Paderborn and Münster.[80] The drastic nature of this decree may be comprehended by the realization that the decree not only forbade the usual ante-nuptial promises as to the up-bringing of the children born of mixed marriages *in futuro,* but also voided any such agreements already entered into in relation to the existing mixed marriages.

The decree immediately provoked bitter and widespread resentment as an official government interference with the parties' rights and as an official endorsement of Protestantism. While the Catholic pastors acceded to the letter of the decree to the extent of refraining from explicitly demanding the guarantees, yet they evaded its requirements in several ways. In the event that the parties themselves failed to give the *cautiones* voluntarily, the pastor refused to publish the banns or to bless the marriage. And in those cases in which a Catholic woman had entered into a mixed marriage without the giving of the *cautiones,* the pastor refused to grant absolution unless the guarantees should be given. Moreover, the pastor refused to allow a married woman to approach the Sacraments if she in fact allowed her children to be brought up in any other than the Catholic religion.

The situation speedily became extremely acute. To avert the rising of unrest and bitterness, Archbishop von Spiegel of Cologne and his suffragan bishops petitioned Frederick William to submit the controversy to the Holy See. Frederick acceded to the request and instructed von Bunsen, his Minister at Rome, to confer with the pontiff on the difficult issue. The negotiations were interrupted by the death of Leo XII, but were re-

[80] A. Knecht, *Handbuch Des Katholischen Eherechts* (Freiburg, Herder & Co., 1928), p. 289.

sumed with his successor, Pius VIII. In 1830, Pius addressed the notable brief, *Litteris Altero,* to the Archbishop of Cologne and the Bishops of Treves, Munster and Paderborn. In his decree, the Roman pontiff reiterated the traditional opposition of the Church to mixed marriages. He further forbade priests to perform any religious ceremony on the occasion of any mixed marriage where the ante-nuptial promises were not given. However, he tolerated mere passive assistance at such ceremonies, admitted the validity of marriages performed without the presence of the parish priest, and refrained from inflicting censures upon Catholics who refused to comply with the canon law requirement demanding such ante-nuptial promises.[81]

Pope Gregory XVI, who succeeded Pius VIII, flatly refused to accede to the demands of the Imperial Government for modifications of the papal decree. The document was transmitted to Berlin in the hands of von Bunsen, and upon its arrival a secret convention was entered into between the Prussian Government and Archbishop Spiegel of Cologne. This was strengthened in turn by an agreement of the bishops with the government. Under such agreement, the papal brief was published, yet it was weakened by a supplementary commentary which set aside the regulatory provisions and yielded to the provisions of the earlier, unpopular imperial decree of 1825. By such action, the bishops made fundamental concessions to the imperial Government in allowing pastors to perform the religious ceremony in mixed marriages without demanding the *cautiones* and in allowing full effect to the earlier decrees' provision which made the father's religion the controlling factor in the religious up-bringing of the offspring of mixed marriages. The reaction to the situation among the rank and file of the clergy and people soon became bitter and rebellious. Stormy scenes followed in rapid succession, including a demand by Gregory XVI for an explanation from von Bunsen, a denial of the agreement by the government, and a courageous

[81] Litt. ap. *Litteris altero,* 25 Mart. 1830—*Fontes,* n. 482.

and loyal stand to enforce the regulations of the Holy See by Archbishop Clemens-Augustus, the successor of von Spiegel in the See of Cologne. Threats by the Prussian Government failed to intimidate him and the government finally resorted to his arrest. Provoked by such hostility, Pope Gregory XVI addressed an allocution to the Cardinals [82] and sent a copy of this protest to each of the Courts of Europe.[83] Pope Gregory further pressed the settlement of the issue in the dioceses of Gnesen-Posen and Breslau, warning the Bishop of the latter, Seldvitzky, concerning reports of his failure to comply with the regulations of the Church in this matter.[84] This was followed by the resignation of that bishop. Frederick William IV (1840-1859), who succeeded Frederick William III, disturbed by the extreme feelings engendered by the long controversy and apprehensive of the general unrest, made peace with the Church and yielded in the vexed mixed marriage question by withdrawing the troublesome government interference.

However, the effects of the earlier decrees persisted in some regions. On June 7, 1853, a drastic army regulation threatened dismissal from the Prussian army of any officer who should dare to comply with the renewed demand of the Church for the promises, supported by any oath, that the *cautiones* would be fulfilled.[85] While in Hungary, the civil laws deemed the promises as valid and binding, yet those laws made the promises enforceable only if affirmed by acknowledgment before a notary.[86] Bavaria likewise recognized the promises as legally binding if affirmed by notarial acknowledgment.[87] In Switzer-

[82] Allocut. *Dum Intima—Acta Greg.* XVI, Vol. II, pp. 237, 238.

[83] Knecht, *op. cit.*, pp. 290 ff.

[84] Allocut. *Officii Memores—Fontes*, n. 492.

[85] Knecht, *op. cit.*, p. 292. See S. C. S. Off., 10 Dec., 1902—*Fontes*, n. 1262.

[86] Knecht, *op. cit.*, p. 295.

[87] Knecht, *op. cit.*, pp. 292, 293.

land, the civil law prescribed that all children of mixed marriages must be reared in the religion of the father. When consulted on the difficult problem in 1863, the Holy See replied that no dispensation could be granted in such cases unless there existed moral certainty of the fulfillment of the promises notwithstanding the hostile provisions of the civil law.[88]

The determined resistance of the Church to efforts of civil powers to undermine the obligation of the promises is revealed in a decision of the Holy Office in 1842.[89] In this decision the Holy See answers in the negative the question whether a mixed marriage can be blessed lawfully where the man is a non-Catholic resident of a territory in which the promises, though voluntarily given, are rendered void by the civil law, which compelled the instruction of the children by Protestant authorities.

Notwithstanding the many and positive decisions requiring the *cautiones,* the effect of old customs persisted to some extent. Some marriages were contracted without the promises being asked or having being requested, were denied. In some of these marriages there existed the impediment of disparity of cult, which necessitated a dispensation for the validity of the marriage. When consulted upon these cases, the Holy See declared them void and further authorized the Ordinary to declare void such marriages, undertaken without the *cautiones,* without the usual requirement of referring the matter to the Holy Office.[90] The drastic wording of this decree has led to a controversy which has persisted even after the Code. The question arose in connection with Canon 1043. This requires the furnishing of the *cautiones* even in those cases in which the law, because of danger of death, relaxes in the usual requirements relating to the form and certain impediments. Does the decision of the Holy See in 1912 bind even in the exceptional circumstances which gave rise to the Canon? If it binds, then

[88] S. C. S. Off. (Helvetiae), 21 ian. 1863—*Fontes,* n. 973.

[89] S. C. S. Off., 30 Jun. 1842—*Fontes,* n. 866.

[90] June 21, 1912—A. A. S., IV (1912), 443.

the *cautiones* must be given. If not given, the dispensation would be invalid, and in cases of disparity of cult the marriage itself would be void.

The authorities are divided upon the subject. One group holds against the strict application of the decree in such circumstances and sponsors the view that the dispensation is valid, provided that the conditions of the divine law are fulfilled and that the Catholic party is well disposed. This group includes O'Keefe,[91] Capello,[92] Petrovits,[93] Motry,[94] Vermeesch-Creusen,[95] Kelly,[96] and Ayrinhac.[97]

The second group holds that the *cautiones* must be given for the validity of the dispensation, even in danger of death. The latter position is maintained by De Smet,[98] Augustine, [99] Schenk,[100] Woywod,[101] Vlaming,[102] and Harrington.[103] Before

[91] G. M. O'Keeffe, *Matrimonial Dispensations* (Washington, Catholic University of America, 1927), pp. 85-92; 144-145.

[92] F. M. Capello, *De Sacramentis* (Turin, Libraria Marietti, 1927), Vol III, n. 310, p. 354.

[93] J. J. C. Petrovits, *The New Church Law on Matrimony* (J. J. McVey, Philadelphia, 1926), n. 160, p. 104.

[94] H. L. Motry, *Diocesan Faculties According to the Code of Canon Law* (Washington, Catholic University of America, 1922), pp. 133-134.

[95] P. A. Vermeersch, *Epitome Iuris Canonici* (Louvain, Museum Lessianum, 1930), n. 306, p. 190.

[96] J. P. Kelly, *The Jurisdiction of the Simple Confessor* (Washington, Catholic University of America, 1927), pp. 92-94, 185.

[97] H. A. Ayrinhac, *Marriage Legislation in the New Code of Canon Law* (New York, Benziger Bros., 1932), p. 69.

[98] A. De Smet, *De Sponsalibus et Matrimonio* (Bruges, C. Bayaert, 1927), n. 505, pp. 504-505.

[99] P. C. Augustine, *A Commentary on the New Code of Canon Law* (St. Louis, B. Herder Co., 1920), Vol. V, pp. 101-102.

[100] *Op. cit.*, p. 227.

[101] S. Woywod, *A Practical Commentary on the Code of Canon Law* (New York, J. F. Wagner, 1925), Vol. I, n. 1011, p. 591.

[102] M. Vlaming, *Praelectiones Iuris Matrimonii* (Bois De Duc, P. Brand, 1919), n. 218, p. 190.

[103] *American Ecclesiastical Review*, Vol. LXV (1921), p. 259.

the decree of 1932 the division of the authorities upon the question made either opinion tenable and gave a solid probability to the more liberal interpretation. However, the decree of 1932 would seem to close authoritatively the question in favor of the strict interpretation. For the wording specifically mentions Canon 1044 which is a further development of Canon 1043. It is addressed not only to the bishop but also to priests, who, in the circumstances described in Canon 1043, namely danger of death and difficulty of approach to the Ordinary, obtain jurisdiction to give certain marital dispensations ordinarily reserved for bishops and the Holy See. It is now well settled that, even in those cases involving danger of death, the *cautiones* must be given.[104]

Such was the historical background in which the commission, appointed in 1904 by the Roman Pontiff,[105] faced the task of codifying the Canon Law. The new law reaffirmed the old traditional belief and discipline of the church as to marriages of her children with those outside the fold.[106] The Code establishes disparity of cult as a diriment impediment [107] which in the absence of dispensation renders the marriage null and void; [108] and mixed marriage as a prohibitive impediment [109] which in the absence of a dispensation, renders the marriage illicit but not invalid.[110]

The power to grant the dispensation lies in the Roman Pontiff. An Ordinary has the right to dispense only by virtue of the power given him by common law or special Apostolic

104 *Ius Pontificium,* XII (1932), Fasc. 1, p. 69.

105 *Motu Proprio,* Pius X, "Arduum sane." March 17, 1904. Acta A. Sedis, Vol. XXXVI, 549.

106 Code of Canon Law, Canons 1060-65, 1070, 1071.

107 Canon 1070.

108 Canon 1036, § 2.

109 Canon 1060, 1061.

110 Canon 1036, § 1, Canon 1038.

indult.[111] Neither can custom, which is so powerful in Canon Law, add to, derogate from, or change impediments [112] and any contrary custom is reprobated.[113] The church prohibits *severissime* mixed marriages because of the ever-present danger of religious perversion of the Catholic party and offspring.[114] Bishops and pastors are required to deter the faithful from such unions.[115] Failing in this, they are to make every endeavor to prevent the breaking of the laws of God and the Church. Further they are required to petition the Ordinary, stating explicitly the reasons for granting the dispensation. Such reasons must constitute a just and grave cause. In certain rare instances however pastors and confessors may dispense. These are certain extreme emergencies embracing only narrowly limited situations such as *in periculo mortis*. But even in these cases the Church requires the cautiones.[116] If the dispensation is granted, the assistance of the pastor is strictly limited as to the ceremony in respect to time, place and manner.[117]

Canon 1061 states that the Church will not give a dispensation, unless for a "just and grave cause," from the impediment of mixed religion, which as has been stated, includes disparity of cult within these provisions. Section 2 demands that:

Can. 1061, § 1, sec. 2.:—*Cautionem praestiterit coniux acatholicus de amovendo a coniuge catholico perversionis periculo, et uterque coniux de universa prole catholice tantum baptizanda et educanda;*

[111] Canon 1040. For faculties of Bishops in United States, see Schenk, *op. cit.*, 166.

[112] Canon 1041.

[113] Canon 1041.

[114] Canon 1060.

[115] Canon 1064.

[116] Canon 1043: "... si dispensatio concedatur super cultus disparitate aut mixta religione, praestitis consuetis cautionibus". For discussion as to the legal import of words by authorities, see Schenk, *op. cit.*, 216 and authorities cited there.

[117] Canon 1102.

Thus the required ante-nuptial promise carries an obligation and a positive undertaking on the part of the non-Catholic spouse " to remove the danger of perversion on the part of the Catholic spouse." The translation of the Latin word "*perversio*" into English is difficult, particularly because the term has acquired in ordinary English usage the connotation of sexual abnormality. The word as used here is not to be thus translated. It is rather to be given a different and larger meaning, which includes any danger which might weaken or destroy the religion of the Catholic party. Religion in this sense includes not only his or her belief, but as well the Catholic's morals, religious practices, and the standards and duties of a Catholic married person as defined by the tradition and authoritative statements of the Church. What " religion " means in this connection may be learned from the ten commandments, particularly the first, second, sixth, ninth, and tenth,[118] and the precepts of the Church, which include not only those known as the first six precepts but all other precepts and regulations. The chief precepts include the duty to hear Holy Mass on Sundays and Holy Days of obligation under pain of sin in the absence of a valid excuse, the duty to keep the fast and abstinence on the appointed days, the duty of approaching the Sacraments of Penance and Holy Eucharist at least once a year, and the duty not only of attending at Church services but as well the obligation to give financial support to the Church in proportion to the individual means of the family.[119] The above requirements give of course only the minimum of the religious duties of the Catholic spouse. Section 2 of Canon 1061 demands a removal by the non-Catholic party of any obstacles to a complete observation of the religious duties of

[118] See P. C. Gasparri, *The Catholic Catechism* (P. J. Kennedy & Sons, New York, 1932), pt. 3, adults, pp. 116-130; Spirago-Clarke, *The Catechism Explained* (Benziger Bros., New York, 1927), pp. 306-332, pp. 339-347, pp. 392-393.

[119] Gasparri, *op. cit.*, pp. 131-138.

the Catholic spouse as an individual and as a Catholic married person.

For a more thorough comprehension of the scope of the non-Catholic promises the reader might profitably consult the noted encyclical of Pope Leo XIII, on Christian Marriage,[120] and the more recent pronouncement of Pope Pius XI, on Christian Marriage.[121] Pope Leo XIII explained the true nature of marriage as an indissoluble union of one man and one woman, (a) for the propagation of the human race "that a people might be born and brought up for the worship and religion of the true God and our Savior, Jesus Christ," and (b) for the mutual solace and comfort of the spouses. The marriage state demands from both spouses the duty of the realization of the holiness of matrimony, faithfulness to the marriage vow, mutual love and sacrifice, the duty of teaching offspring the duties of obedience to parents and respect for authority, the Christian education of the children, and the equal burden of patient and Christian fortitude in the occasional disappointments, worries and hardships of every married life. Pope Pius XI, after reviewing with praise the encyclical of Pope Leo XIII, vindicates the noble nature and high dignity of the marriage state as a "partnership in life," the chief blessing of which is children, and the essential virtues of which are "unity, chastity, charity and honorable obedience." The pontiff then strikes powerfully at the modern errors concerning marriage, and includes in those errors, writings, theatrical productions, novels, motion pictures and radio broadcasts in which "the sanctity of marriage is trampled upon and derided, divorce, adultery, and all the basest vices are either extolled or at least depicted—free from all reprovals and infamy." He further assails the philosophy which would make naturalism

[120] Encyclical Letter, "Christian Marriage," *Great Encyclical Letters of Leo XIII* (New York, Benziger Bros., 1903), p. 58.

[121] Encyclical Letter, "Christian Marriage," *Four Great Encyclicals* (New York, The Paulist Press, 1932), p. 73.

the basis of marriage and scores the evils of companionate marriage and the prevalent and grave abuse of contraceptive birth control. In regard to the latter, he states that no difficulty, however great, can justify such practice because it is "an offense against the law of God and of nature, and those who indulge in such are branded with the guilt of a grave sin." A variety of positive hindrances to the religious belief and practices of the Catholic can be easily enumerated from the above exposition. They would include the practice of birth control, the possession or reading of forbidden books, the attendance at performances at which lax morals are portrayed, and the joining of forbidden societies. In brief, the non-Catholic undertakes to remove any hindrances to the faith or the performance of the moral and religious duties of the Catholic which are contrary to the duties as outlined in these able and clear expositions by the Holy See.

The second part of Canon 1061, section 2, requires that both the Catholic and non-Catholic spouses promise to baptize and educate all the children in the Catholic religion exclusively. The obligation relating to baptism is clear in its wording. The obligation relating to the education of the children requires an understanding of the meaning of the term "education" in the Catholic sense. For it embraces far more than mere mental instruction and includes as well religious and moral training. Pope Pius XI, in the Encyclical Letter, on the Christian Education of youth,[122] exposes the fundamental error of modern theorists who "pretend to draw education out of human nature itself and evolve it by its own unaided powers." Such theorists easily fall into error because "instead of fixing their gaze on God, first principle and last end of the whole universe, they fall back upon themselves, becoming attached exclusively to passing things of earth. . ." He continues, "it is clear that there can be no true education which is not wholly directed to

[122] Encyclical Letter of Pius XI, on "Christian Education of Youth" (National Catholic Welfare Conference, Washington, D. C., 1930).

man's last end . . ." and, "there can be no ideally perfect education which is not Christian education." He vindicates the Church in the field of educational training and points out that She not only does not interfere with society but confers "valuable assistance in the right ordering and well-being of families and of civil society; for it keeps far away from youth the moral poison which at that inexperienced and changeable age more easily penetrates the mind and more rapidly spreads its baneful effects." He cites the provisions of the Canon Law, can. 1113: "Parents are under a most grave obligation to see to the religious and moral education of their children, as well as to their physical and civic training, as far as they can, and moreover to provide for their temporal well-being." He points out the duties of parents to refuse to send their children "to those schools in which there is danger of imbibing the deadly poison of impiety." He outlines the true scope of the parents' duty as "The obligation of the family to bring up children includes not only religious and moral education, but physical and civic education as well, principally insofar as it touches upon religion and morality." Parents are warned to teach discipline and correct the mistakes and evil tendencies of their children, and to point out the strong teaching derived from adherence to supernatural truth and from the channels of grace in the Sacraments of the Church. He condemns the modern fallacies of pedagogic naturalism, indiscreet sex education, and other errors. He calls attention to the Church law requiring attendance at Catholic schools, and lays stress upon the benefits to children "received in a well-ordered and well-disciplined Christian family;" which is "more efficacious in proportion to the clear and constant good example set, first by the parents, and then by the other members of the household." He stresses as well the need of watchfulness over the recreations and unoccupied hours of youth.

He finally epitomizes the meaning of this Christian education as one which "takes in the whole aggregate of human life, physical and spiritual, intellectual and moral, individual, domestic and social, not with a view of reducing it in any way, but in order to elevate, regulate and perfect it, in accordance with the example and teaching of Christ."

Canon 1061 makes evident the weighty appraisal which the Church places upon the obligations contained in the ante-nuptial promises.

Canon 1061, § 1, Sec. 3: *Moralis habeatur certitudo de cautionum implemento.*

Thus the Church law demands moral certainty of the fulfillment of the promises in the authority which dispenses, usually the Ordinary. And it is generally held that this requirement must be fulfilled under the heavy penalty of rendering the dispensation invalid in its absence.[123] "Moral certitude" in this particular usage refers to the term as used in the moral theology of the Church. It is not objective in the sense of conforming to objective reality. It is rather a subjective norm, governed however by objective criteria. This "moral certainty" has been variously defined as "that certainty which excludes every positive, grave, and prudent doubt";[124] as "a prudent certainty which does not exclude all doubt but only any prudent doubt."[125] Negatively, it has been described as that certitude which is beyond "a mere probability or some hope or a mere conjecture or hope of fulfillment."[126] The evidence upon which such a moral certainty may rest may arise from different sources. Among the criteria of the probability of fulfillment of the ante-nuptial promises may be listed the following: the

[123] F. Ter Haar (Connell), *Mixed Marriages and Their Remedies* (New York, F. Pustet & Co., 1933); Schenk, *op. cit.*, p. 247.

[124] Ter Haar, *op. cit.*, pp. 84-96.

[125] A. Tanquerey, *Synopsis Theologiae Moralis* (Rome, Desclee, 1922), n. 368, p. 212.

[126] F. M. Cappello, *De Sacramentis* (Turin, Marietti, 1927), Vol. III, n. 311, p. 355.

character of the Catholic, the character and reputation of the non-Catholic, the courtship before marriage, the attitude of the non-Catholic during the preliminary religious instructions, the age and circumstances, and history of the parties, particularly if married before.[127]

The requirement of the solemn and formal agreement by both parties has undoubtedly been very helpful in securing the performance of the promises in many cases. But it has been far from completely successful, either in guaranteeing the sincere intention of the signers or the subsequent fulfillment of the promises. It seems clear that sometimes one party or both execute[128] the agreement in deceit, having an affirmative intention of not living up to their signed promises. They apparently intend solely to go through the pantomime of compliance with canonical requirements in order to secure the desired dispensation from the Church.

How far does this lack of sincerity affect the validity of the marriage based upon it? Does the fraud upon the Church and the dispensing authority render the dispensation void? The answer to the question becomes vitally important. In the case of mixed marriage, if the dispensation is void because of such fraud, it would render the marriage gravely illicit though not invalid. On the contrary, in the case of a marriage in which there is disparity of cult, if the fraud renders the dispensation void, then in turn the marriage resting upon such dispensation would be null and void. The question, particularly under this last phase, has been warmly disputed by canonists and persists now as a moot question in eminent theological and canonical reviews.

At the outset of any consideration of this particular question, to wit: How far does the lack of sincerity in the *cautiones* affect

[127] Ter Haar, *op. cit.*, pp. 90-93; Vlaming, *Praelectiones Iuris Matrimonii* (Bois de Duc, P. Brand, 1919), n. 219, 191.

[128] The word "execute" is used throughout in the accepted legal sense "to make a document by the required signing."

the validity of the dispensation?—the reader should sharply distinguish between two types of situations which arise in this connection. The first type of situation arises where the sincerity of the maker of the promises is placed by the other party as *a true condition precedent to the giving of the marriage consent* by the latter. This situation provokes a study which lies deeper than the considerations of the canonical requirements of Canon 1061. The discussion leads to the very essence of marriage, namely, the marital consent. Some confuse the consideration of this question by alleging the improbability of such a condition of the marital consent, or raise the difficulty of proving that this was made a true condition, or fear the fact that the answer might be used to open the door to fraud. In spite of such objections and difficulties, the answer to the question is clear and well-settled. If it is proven as a juridical fact that the sincere execution of the promises was a true condition to the marital consent and the condition was not fulfilled, then the marital consent was not present and there was no marriage. In other words, if the court finds that the marital consent of the promisee was contingent upon the sincerity of the promisor in the giving of the *cautiones*—then the marital consent, so conditioned, never arises in the absence of the demanded sincerity. And such a marriage, whether it be with dispensation from the impediment of mixed marriage or the impediment of disparity of cult, would fail because of the absence of true marital consent. Such a marriage would be null and void, and the solution is admitted by all authorities.[129]

The second type of situation arises where the sincerity of one party has not been posited as a condition precedent to the giving of the marital consent by the other party. And thus the question in this type of situation concerns itself solely with the mind of the law-giver and the granting power of the dispensation. How far will the lack of sincerity affect the dis-

[129] S. Roman Rota, 26 Nov. 1921—A. A. S., XIV (1922), p. 515 ff.

pensation? It may be worth while to set out here the exact text of Canon 1061.

> I. *Ecclesia super impedimento mixtae religionis non dispensat, nisi:*
>
> 1. *Urgeant justae ac graves causae;*
> 2. *Cautionem praestiterit conjux acatholicus de amovendo a conjuge catholico perversionis periculo, et uterque conjux de universa prole catholice tantum baptizanda et educanda;*
> 3. *Moralis habeatur certitudo de cautionum implemento.*
>
> II. *Cautiones regulariter in scriptis exigantur.*

It must be admitted at the outset that the canon does not contain any express requirement of sincerity in *ipsis verbis.* But that objection falls far short of providing any conclusive answer to our question. Some eminent canonists, notably Gasparri and Capello [130] do not treat the question. Others complicate the determination of the question by combining the original question under consideration, namely, " How far does the lack of sincerity affect the validity of the dispensation? ", with a further question, " And how is the answer made dependent upon the determination of the moral certainty of the dispensing authority in the particular case? "

This manner of treatment seems to unnecessarily add difficulties to the solution of the problem. Apart from the question of sincerity, the canon demands a subjective moral certainty on the part of the dispensing authority that the *cautiones* will be fulfilled. The canon goes still further and requires moral certainty for the *validity* of the dispensation. That criterion, namely, the presence or absence of moral certainty in the Ordinary, is effective in determining many cases. But in many other cases, the Ordinary may well have subjective moral certainty where *in fact* the party or parties executing the *cautiones* may have executed them with a lack of intention

[130] Gasparri, *De Matrimonio.*
Capello, *De Sacramentis,* Vol. III.

concerning their fulfillment. Thus the question presented is narrower than: " What effect will ensue from insincerity plus a lack of subjective moral certainty? " The question is rather, in its simplest terms: " What effect has the lack of sincerity upon a dispensation in cases of mixed marriages or disparity of cult? "

The recent study of the *Ius Pontificium*,[131] which holds that lack of sincerity in the *cautiones* does not render the dispensation invalid, has awakened new interest in a question which had provoked violent discussion a decade earlier. At that time, O'Donnell, writing in the *Irish Ecclesiastical Record*,[132] had upheld the same view. O'Donnell argued that, had the Church intended that insincerity would produce so drastic a result as to render the dispensation and marriage invalid (if the dispensation was given in disparity of cult) the Church would have specifically legislated to that end. And he pointed out that such a result could have been accomplished easily by simple changes and additions in wording. He further sought to fortify his own position by a negative argument. It is drawn from an examination of official documents relating to *cautiones*, in which he found that the subjective sincerity of the parties was nowhere stressed, but rather that the emphasis was placed upon the moral certainty of the dispensing authority in the fulfillment of the promises. From this absence, he concluded that sincerity of the party executing the *cautiones* was not a condition precedent to the validity of the dispensation. O'Donnell's interpretation was sharply challenged by J. C. Harrington in the *American Ecclesiastical Review*.[133] He asserted that " Promises made in bad faith are equivalent to none at all ", and decried the opposite opinion as putting " a premium on dishonesty " and " tantamount to encouraging

[131] *Ius Pontificium*, XIII (1933), 207-214.

[132] *Irish Ecclesiastical Record*, XVIII (1921), 411-418.

[133] J. C. Harrington, *American Ecclesiastical Review*, LXV (1921), 257-262.

fraud and fictitious consent to procure the end desired, viz, marriage in the Church with the Catholic party." L. P. Foley, writing later in the *Homiletic and Pastoral Review*,[184] renewed the controversy, rejecting the earlier opinion of the *Irish Ecclesiastical Record*, and holding strongly that the lack of sincerity renders void the dispensation. He asserted that the only authority cited for the contrary opinion is that earlier authority of the *Irish Ecclesiastical Record*, given above. However, he neglected to consider the presence of a few, yet eminent, canonists, such as Vromant,[185] De Smet[186] and De Becker,[187] who differ with him and agree with the opinion that the dispensation remains valid. The writer weakens the reader's confidence in his conclusion by a noticeable weakness in citation of authority and a marked boldness in sweeping statements. The discussion is not aided by roundly condemning his opponent for the opinion "that a completely concealed intention *in no way* affects the validity of an outward act." Validity does not lend itself to being affected in a variety of ways or degrees, lesser or greater. The dispensation affected by the lack of sincerity is simply valid or not valid. The writer's criticism continues, "In this he goes against *all existing jurisprudence*, which clearly holds that a fictitious act is no act. . . ." This, of course, reaches far beyond any proper limits, and is not true in that sweeping sense, at least in Anglo-American jurisprudence.[188] He further cites Canon 45 under which a false *final* cause in the dispensation renders such dispensation invalid. But that canon includes the added words, "*si falsa causa finalis eaque unica proponatur.*" And it cannot

[184] L. P. Foley, "Sincerity of the Promises Before Mixed Marriages", *The Homiletic and Pastoral Review*, XXXIII (1933), 742-743.

[185] Vromant, *De Matrimonio*, n. 166.

[186] De Smet, *De Sponsalibus et Matrimonio*, n. 505, 590, 874.

[187] L. De Becker, *De Matrimonio* (Louvain: Fr. Ceuterick, 1931).

[188] Williston, *Contracts*, Vol. II, Sects. 663 ff., pp. 1279 ff.; Vol. III, Sect 1494, p. 2658.

fairly be maintained that the *cautiones* come within the meaning of *causa* Canon 45. Continuing, he proceeds to strengthen his conclusion by *a fortiori* reasoning because, he asserts, this is a matter of dispensing not from ecclesiastical but from Divine Law, which forbids mixed marriage unless the danger of perversion is removed; and it is not in fact removed by insincere promises.[139] Not a single authority is cited for the last proposition. Now the question of the exact nature of the underlying basis for the requirement of the *cautiones* has not been set out authoritatively to the minute extent of an exact analysis and definition of the limits of Divine Law and ecclesiastical law. It is clear that the impediment of mixed marriage and the legislation providing for the granting of a dispensation in certain cases coming under specified conditions, is of "natural and Divine law" and as well "of Divine Law and ecclesiastical law."[140] It is easily understood that the absence of "*Contumelia Creatoris*" and the removal of the "*periculum perversionis*" are required by Divine Law. And while it is true that the execution of the *cautiones* always is of great practical importance and is also required by the law-maker for validity in the granting of such a dispensation, yet it must be remembered that the execution of the promises is not the only possible method of accomplishing the desired result, to wit: the avoidance of *Contumelia Creatoris* and the removal of the *periculum perversionis*.[141] There is no question that there can exist and, *de facto*, do exist many cases where the dangers are removed without the actual execution of the *cautiones*. Clearly then, the so-called *a fortiori* reasoning does not justify the broad conclusion derived in part from an unjustified premise that removal of danger of perversion depends absolutely upon

139 *Op. cit.*, p. 743.

140 *Decree on Ante-Nuptial Promises in Mixed Marriages, supra*, n. 1; see text, *infra*, p. 40.

141 Gasparri, *De Matrimonio*, Vol. I, n. 439, 440, 450. Capello, *De Sacramentis*, Vol. III, n. 307, 309, 425.

execution of sincere ante-nuptial promises.[142] Such extremely broad statements do not lead the critical reader to agreement, regardless of his feeling that the conclusion itself is correct.

The *Ius Pontificium,* after reviewing the history and nature of marriage dispensations, concludes that the dispensation, in disparity of cult cases, (a) relaxes the ecclesiastical law, by the force of which the marriage would have been otherwise void, and (b) removes, through the solemn execution of the *cautiones,* the basis of the prohibitive impediment of the natural law so that the prohibition of the Divine Law no longer urges. The writer contends that the dispensation is valid even in the face of lack of sincerity in the execution of the solemn promises. He asserts that the Church could not reasonably posit the validity of a dispensation from a mere ecclesiastical law and the validity of the marriage contract itself upon such an imperceptible and variable element as internal intention. The writer fails to allege any authoritative decrees in support of his contention that lack of sincerity does not render the dispensation null. His emphasis upon the absence of the word "*sincerae*" or its equivalent in the formula of rescript from the Holy Office falls far short of proof that such absence indicates that insincere promises will fulfill the canonical requirements. And in the same way, the citation from Vlaming,[143] in which the latter reassures the Ordinary of the reasonable limits to be placed upon an enquiry in obtaining moral certainty, fails to strengthen his position on the precise question at issue. The assertion that the execution of the *cautiones* is demanded by law to remove the *periculum insinceritatis* is hardly an adequate statement of the purpose. And even if it were, it does not justify the final conclusion of the author, that the law-giver does not render the dispensation invalid, where vitiated by a lack of sincerity, but prefers to rely upon its power of moral

[142] Gasparri, *op. cit.*, Vol. I, n. 450. Schenk, *op. cit.*, n. 334.

[143] Ius Pontificium, *op. cit.*, p. 211, quoting, Vlaning (Praelect. Iuris Matrim., II, n. 482).

persuasion of both, its power of punishment over the Catholic party, and upon the power of the vague *conscientia publica* to induce fulfillment of such insincere promises.

The *Homiletic and Pastoral Review*,[144] as has been said, *The Irish Ecclesiastical Record*,[145] differing from its earlier writer, O'Donnell, and *The Ecclesiastical Review* [146] disagree with the *Ius Pontificium* on this issue. All hold that the lack of sincerity nullifies the dispensation, and in cases of disparity of cult, renders the marriage void as well. They are supported in their position by some strong authorities, including Petrovits,[147] Woywod,[148] and Nau.[149] Ayrinhac-Lydon,[150] and O'Neil,[151] Schenk [152] and Ayrinhac-Lydon [153] review the claims of the opponents in the controversy and come to the conclusion that the lack of sincerity does not render the dispensation void; or in any event, according to Ayrinhac-Lydon, does not justify a decree of nullity without referring the matter to the Holy Office. The former lays great emphasis upon the historical evidence of the role of the *cautiones* through several centuries and concludes that the formalities were rather guides to de-

144 L. P. Foley, *The Homiletic and Pastoral Review*, XXXIII (1933), 742-743.

145 *Irish Ecclesiastical Record*, LXIX (1933), 630-635.

146 *The Ecclesiastical Review*, XC, no. 2, "Second Marriage Ceremony before a Minister", 173. See pp. 174, 175.

147 J. J. C. Petrovits, *The New Church Law on Matrimony* (2nd ed., Philadelphia: J. J. McVey, 1926), n. 257, p. 193.

148 Woywod, *A Practical Commentary on The Code of Canon Law* (New York, J. F. Wagner, 1925), I, n. 1056, p. 627.

149 Nau, *Manual on the Marriage Laws of Canon Law* (New York, F. Pustet Co., 1933), p. 72.

150 Ayrinhac-Lydon, *Marriage Legislation in the New Code of Canon Law* (New York, Benziger Bros., 1932).

151 W. H. O'Neil, *Papal Rescripts of Favor* (Washington, Catholic University of America, 1930), 115, note 60.

152 F. Schenk, *Mixed Religion and Disparity of Cult* (Washington, Catholic University of America, 1929), 254.

153 *Op. cit.*, p. 108.

termine the proper granting of a dispensation than conditions precedent to its validity. As stated earlier, De Smet, Vromant, and De Becker [154] hold that the lack of sincerity would not invalidate this dispensation. To the writer, it seems that the opinion, under which lack of sincerity renders null the dispensation is preferable. To determine, then, the mind of the law-maker, we consider the general principles of interpretation and, in particular, those principles which apply to dispensations and rescripts. It seems most important, however, to further consider carefully the whole text of the canon, of which this particular requirement is a part. To be sure, it must be admitted that the canon does not require sincerity for validity *in ipsis verbis.*

As has been said, Canon 45 has been quoted as an authority in aiding the determination of the question. This canon provides:

> Can. 45.—*Cum rescriptis ad preces alicuius impetratis apponitur clasula: Motu proprio, valent quidem ea, si in precibus reticeatur veritas alioquin necessario exprimenda, non tamen si falsa causa finalis eaque unica proponatur, salvo praescripto* can. 1054.

This cannot solve the problem, for the dispensations in these cases are not given with the clause "*motu proprio*" nor are *cautiones* a *causa.*

Nor does Canon 1054 aid the solution:

> Can. 1054.—*Dispensatio a minore impedimento concessa, nullo sive obreptionis sive subreptionis vitio irritatur, etsi unica causa finalis in precibus exposita falsa fuerit.*

For this canon is applicable only in cases of minor impediments, while those in mixed marriage and disparity of cult are major impediments.[155]

[154] *Supra*: see n. 7, n. 8, n. 8a.

[155] *Code of Canon Law,* Canon 1042; W. H. O'Neil, *Papal Rescripts of Favor* (Washington, Catholic University of America, 1930), pp. 132 ff.; Gasparri, *op. cit.*, Vol. I, n. 211, p. 129.

Nor can the problem be solved by the wording of Canon 39, which prescribes, that in rescripts, only those conditions may be considered as essential for the validity of the rescript as are expressly indicated by such words as " si " and " dummodo ".

But Canon 39 and the other canons governing rescripts cannot determine this question. For the petition for the dispensation in mixed marriage cases and the dispensation itself cannot be brought within the fundamental definition of a rescript.[156]

We are driven then to a further consideration of the nature of the dispensation and a further examination of the complete text of the canon governing the granting of the dispensation.

A dispensation may be defined as " an act whereby, in a particular case, a lawful superior grants relaxation from an existing law." [157] A matrimonial dispensation may be defined as " a legitimate act of a superior by which the obligation prohibiting marriage, with or without the nullity of the contract, is relaxed in a particular case." [158] Thus the marriage dispensation is a relaxation of the general law in a particular case, while the general law remains in force for the community at large. It differs from abrogation and derogation because these latter suppress the law itself in part or *in toto;* and it differs from epikeia, which supposes that the law-maker " did not intend to include a particular case within the scope of his law." [159]

" Hence it is said that the *raison d'être* for the dispensation lies in the nature of prudent administration, which often counsels the adapting of general legislation to the needs of a particular case by way of exception. The divine purpose of the Church, the welfare of souls, obliges her to reconcile

156 E. G. Roelker, *Principles of Privilege According to the Code of Canon Law* (Washington, Catholic University of America, 1926), p. 21.

157 *Code of Canon Law.* Canon 80.

158 G. M. O'Keeffe, *Matrimonial Dispensations; Powers of Bishops, Priests, and Confessors* (Washington, Catholic University of America, 1927), p. 3.

159 O'Keefe, *op. cit.*, p. 4.

as far as possible the general interests of the community with the spiritual needs or even weaknesses of its individual members." [160] A dispensation is a *vulnus legis,* and some justifying reason is necessary to compensate for such a wound. A just reason is always required for the lawful granting of a dispensation, even on the part of the legislator. And an inferior is bound to the existence of such a just reason not only for the liceity of the dispensation but as well for its very validity.[161] The Canon Law provides that the Church does not dispense in cases of mixed marriage and disparity of cult unless the non-Catholic spouse gives a promise to remove all danger of perversion to the faith of the Catholic spouse, and both spouses must give a promise to baptize and bring up all the children in the Catholic faith.

The canon further requires that the *cautiones* must be *regulariter* reduced to writing.[162] The most significant phase of the canon, for our consideration of this problem, is the canon's drastic requirement of moral certainty of the fulfillment of the promises in the mind of the dispensing authority.[163] This moral certainty is demanded for the validity of the dispensation itself. This is clear law.[164] Even in the *presence of good faith* on the part of the spouses themselves, the dispensation would be *invalid* if the dispensing power lacked the required moral certainty of their fulfillment. It can hardly be maintained that the law-maker, in this same canon setting such a severe requirement for validity, intended to accept in answer to its demand for a solemn written promise, a sham agreement lacking sincerity. And it seems contrary to the whole purpose

[160] O'Keeffe, *op. cit.*, p. 2.

[161] *Code of Canon Law.* Canon 84, 1.

[162] *Code of Canon Law.* Canon 1061, 2.

[163] *Code of Canon Law.* Canon 1061, 31, n. 3.

[164] De Becker, *op. cit.*, 92; Cappello, *op. cit.*, Vol. III, Sect. 310; Schenk, *op. cit.*, pp. 251 ff.; Ius Pontificium, *supra*, 211; *The Ecclesiastical Review,* XC, 2 (1934), 174; O'Neil, *Rescripts of Favor, supra*, 114.

and spirit of the canon to hold that the Church, laying down such safeguards, would posit a valid dispensation upon such compliance, amounting to a mere pantomine of fraud in a matter that is required as evidence of the removal of a hindrance and of a danger, that is offensive to both divine and natural law, and which gives evidence of the fulfillment of a condition which will justify the dispensation as a "*vulnus legis*".

In this stage of the settlement of this difficult problem, it would seem unwarranted for any inferior authority to presume to adjudicate the matter without referring it to the Holy See for final determination.

Canon 1062 places an additional obligation upon the Catholic party to use prudent efforts to effect the conversion of the non-Catholic party to the Catholic faith. The obligation is based upon the divine and natural obligation of Charity. Its purpose is the conversion of the non-Catholic party to the Church founded by Christ. The practical desirability of such conversion is manifest in that it secures the necessary unity of thought and harmony in religious practice which is essential to the right living and proper bringing-up of the children. The obligation, however, is to be fulfilled in a prudent manner and to be achieved more by prayer, good example, and persuasion which will not divide and antagonize the desired harmony of family life.

The strictness of the present universal law under the Code represents a great step forward in the progress of Church Law. Indeed, it represents the triumph of an uniform, universal regulation over diverse customs and practices which had hampered and confused the situation to some extent through centuries. While the new Code was effective in accomplishing the desired discipline to some extent, the evil of mixed marriages continued to become more serious, particularly in countries predominantly non-Catholic. The legal standing of the *cautiones* in the Civil law was of course unaffected by the Canon law provisions, and the situation prior to the Code, continued to exist. According to the Civil law requirements, in some states, the Civil law was disinclined to enforce them or even placed obstacles in the way of their fulfillment.

The situation was further complicated in some places by the laxity of ecclesiastical authorities in failing to require the giving of the promises or in drafting them in a careless and faulty way. A certain bishop, exasperated by prevalent abuses in matrimonial matters, petitioned the Supreme Sacred Congregation of the Holy Office. He stated that the civil law in his territory gave legal recognition to the promises if they were made with the formalities required by the state for other contracts, viz., acknowledgment before a notary public and two witnesses. He therefore appealed to the Supreme Sacred Congregation of the Holy Office to require the making of these promises in his diocese in such a manner as to ensure legal recognition and impose such obligation upon ecclesiastical authorities *ad validitatem*.[165] The Holy Office granted the request in a general decree on the fourteenth day of January, 1932, when the Holy Office issued the following:

DECREE ON ANTE-NUPTIAL PROMISES IN MIXED MARRIAGES

It sometimes happens that so-called mixed marriages between a Catholic and a non-Catholic, whether baptized or not baptized, are contracted, after the required guarantees are given indeed, but in such a manner that their fulfillment, especially as regards the Catholic education of the offspring of both sexes, cannot effectively be enforced in some regions because the civil laws oppose it; or even that it can be easily hindered by a local secular authority or an heretical minister, even against the will of the parents.

Lest so important a precept of natural and divine law be frustrated to the great detriment of innocent souls, the Most Eminent and Most Reverend Cardinals charged with safeguarding the integrity of faith and morals, in a plenary meeting held Wednesday, the

[165] F. Bernardini, "Decree respecting ante-nuptial agreements," *Eccles. Review*, LXXXVIII (1933), 185, 186.

thirteenth day of January, 1932, having also in mind our Holy Father's recent encyclical letter beginning *Casti connubii,* considered it their strict duty to call the attention of all Bishops and likewise of pastors and others mentioned in canon 1044, who are empowered to dispense from the impediments of mixed religion and disparity of cult, and to oblige them in conscience never to grant such dispensations, unless the couple to be married first give the guarantees, the faithful fulfillment of which no one can hinder, not even by the force of the civil laws to which one or the other may be subject and which are in force in the place of their present residence or (if it be foreseen that they may perhaps betake themselves elsewhere) in the place of their future residence; otherwise the dispensation itself shall be wholly null and invalid.

On Thursday, however, the fourteenth day of the same month and year, our Holy Father Pius XI, by Divine Providence Pope, confirmed this resolution of the Most Eminent Fathers and ordered it to be published, commanding that those concerned shall observe it and see to it that it is observed.[166]

Thus the decree re-affirmed the traditional attitude of the Church in the matter of ante-nuptial promises as embodied in the provisions of the new code of Canon law.

The interpretation of the decree as to the extent of its application *ad validatem dispensationis* has been vigorously debated by canonical authorities.

The drastic effect of the decree appeared most strikingly in its concluding clause which rendered dispensations, granted contrary to its prescriptions, "*wholly null and invalid.*" This statement awakened tremendous public interest particularly because of the sensational misinterpretations of the decree by the secular press. According to some despatches, the decree rendered void those mixed marriages, hitherto valid, if the promises relative to the Catholic upbringing of the children

[166] *Acta Apostolicae Sedis,* XXIV (1932), 15. This translation was made by the Rev. Valentine Schaaf, O.F.M., J.C.D., professor of Canon Law at the Catholic University of America. Latin text will be found in Appendix, p. 145.

had not been fulfilled.[167] The public was naturally shocked at the inconsistency of a once valid marriage being rendered void because of the contingent happening of events afterwards. Canonists soon corrected such patently erroneous interpretations. But the unusual severity of the decree, rendering the dispensation void in cases of mixed marriage, and rendering void both the dispensation and the marriage itself in cases of disparity of cult—created immediate and unusual interest concerning the applicability of the decree in the United States. The question had far deeper significance than mere academic discussion. For upon its determination depended the validity of many future dispensations to be granted in this country, where the numbers of mixed marriages have continued to show an appalling increase.

Does the decree apply *ad validitatem* to the United States? Canonists differ in the answer, and vary even in their reasoning leading up to identical conclusions. With the same mature reasoning exhibited by him in his long and varied canonical studies and experience, the eminent authority Gasparri narrated the particular circumstances leading up to the decree in question. He stated that the petition made known to the Holy See that the civil authorities in some territories gave legal enforceability to the *cautiones,* if those promises should be given in a manner and a form determined and approved by the civil law. In that situation, the Holy Office rightly decreed that no dispensations should be granted in *those regions* unless the *cautiones* should be given in that particular form prescribed by the law in that particular place.[168] Such an interpretation would lead one to the conclusion that the decree does not apply *ad validitatem* in the United States, because no state provides by statute for the legal enforceability of the promises if the parties execute them in any particular form or manner. Bernardini agrees with Gasparii and explains his opinion in

[167] See references under n. 2, *supra.*

[168] *De Matrimonio,* Vol. I, n. 455, pp. 269 ff.

the *American Ecclesiastical Review*.[169] There he says, (1) " In territory where it is possible to have the ante-nuptial agreements recognized by the state—when made in accordance with the form prescribed by the civil law—the ante-nuptial agreements should be made in accordance with said legally required form, under penalty of nullity. . . . (2) In territory where legislation . . . nullifies such ante-nuptial agreements, or refuses to recognize that they may form the object of a true civil contract—the decree does not affect anew the validity of such dispensations. (3) In territory where possibility of legal recognition is doubtful . . . the decree does not apply *ad validitatem*. . . . In conclusion, it seems clear that until such time as the enforceability of the ante-nuptial contract is favorably established by legal precedent or by statutory enactment, the decree . . . does not apply anywhere in the United States." De Becker,[170] Schaaf,[171] Nau,[172] Ter Haar-Connell,[173] Kearney,[174] and Ayrinhac-Lydon[175] agree with the conclusion of Bernardini that the decree does not apply *ad validitatem* in the United States. Schaaf, Nau and Ayrinhac-Lydon further express the opinion that if positive hostile laws should prevent the enforcement, then the decree would apply *ad validitatem*. However, as Dr. Schaaf points out, such a legal situation would indicate conditions in which

169 P. Bernardini, *American Ecclesiastical Review*, LXXXVIII (1933), 185, 190.

170 J. De Becker, *Ephemerides Theologicae Lovanienses*, X (1933), 654-658.

171 V. T. Schaaf, *American Ecclesiastical Review*, LXXXVI (1932), 408-412.

172 L. J. Nau, *Manual on the Marriage Laws of the Code of Canon Law* (New York, F. Pustet Co., 1933), pp. 71 ff.

173 F. Ter Haar–F. J. Connell, *Mixed Marriages and Their Remedies* (New York, F. Pustet Co., 1933), pp. 185-195.

174 R. A. Kearney, "A Recent Decree on Mixed Marriages," *Quarterly Bulletin of the International Federation of Catholic Alumnae*, XV (1932), 15-17.

175 H. Ayrinhac–P. J. Lydon, *Marriage Legislation in the New Code of Canon Law* (New York, Benziger Bros., 1932), p. 110.

the fundamental requirement of canon law, apart from this decree demanding moral certainty, could not be fulfilled in the usual case. Under such a view, this decree places an added positive prohibition over and above the previous prescriptions of the general law. Woywod hesitates to express a certain opinion in the matter and feels that a clarification of meaning is needed before a definite decision can be given. He stresses, however, the circumstances leading to the decree and seems to indicate that, as yet, the decree would be restricted in operation to those countries where positive adverse laws existed which would exclude the moral certainty of the fulfillment of the promises.[176]

Dr. P. O'Neill of Maynooth[177] one of the foremost authorities for the stricter view that the decree applies *ad validitatem,* reasons that any dispensation granted by Ordinaries in the present situation of the law would be void. O'Neill states his views in the *Irish Ecclesiastical Record* and considers the application of the decree to a common-law country such as Ireland. The conclusion would apply to England and the United States, as well as to Scotland, Canada and Australia, because all have inherited the system of common law.[178] O'Neill disregards the important elements of such an analysis as Gasparri's. O'Neill neglects to give due consideration to the important fact that in the circumstances of the instant case the law gave the promises legal effect if executed in a certain manner and form. He refers to the less severe interpretation of the applicability of the decree by Jombart and rests his opinion chiefly upon two allegations. First, he extracts certain words from the decree and emphasizes them, claiming to give them a literal meaning, and, secondly, he stresses heavily his claim that other interpretations than his render the decree simply a reiteration of the

[176] *Homiletic Review,* XXXII (1933), pp. 755 ff.

[177] *Irish Ecclesiastical Record,* XXXIX (1932), 532 ff.

[178] This applies with the notable exception of a state such as Louisiana, which follows the Continental Code instead of the Common Law.

general law embodied in the Code.[179] The first condition seems unsound because, as Gasparri points out, the original complaint by the bishop concerned the failure to require the execution of the promises in the certain manner and form in which the civil law granted legal enforceability. The second claim may be challenged with some force by pointing out its error. The general law never legislated, requiring that the *cautiones* must be executed *ad validitatem* in that particular manner of several modes, which would give the agreement legal enforceability. To be sure, that manner of executing the *cautiones* which obtained the sanction of the law would be the more prudent choice, and would seem to indicate more clearly the moral certainty of their fulfillment. But it positively cannot be said that other modes of executing the promises would not produce moral certainty in many cases. If the view of Gasparri and the weight of authority be taken that the decree applies *ad validitatem* only to those territories in which the execution of the *cautiones* in a *certain manner* will carry legal enforceability —then this decree, which demands that particular manner of execution, goes far in supplementing the general law previously existing in such territories. And further, the circumstances which gave rise to this decree constituted exactly such a situation.

The Irish Ecclesiastical Record, in a later article, expresses the opinion that the distinguished Canonist, Maroto, confirms their earlier interpretation as to the applicability of the decree.[180] Postponing temporarily an analysis of the opinion of Maroto, we may proceed to consider the extremely significant reply contained in the article, which is the answer of the Holy Office to an Irish Bishop who sought further authentic information in answer to the question concerning the applicability of the decree. In the particular answer given to the Irish bishop, the Holy Office intimated that the decree applies only to those ter-

179 *Op. cit.*, p. 534.

180 *Irish Ecclesiastical Record,* Vol. XL, no. 5 ff., p. 409 ff.

ritories where the civil law gives legal effect to the promises. This would seem to be contrary to the earlier interpretation of O'Neill in the *Irish Ecclesiastical Record*. The opinion of Jombart, rejected by the *Irish Ecclesiastical Record,* appeared in the Nouvelle Revue Theologique.[181] Jombart admits that the text of the decree might justify such an extremely severe interpretation as was placed by the *Irish Ecclesiastical Record,* to wit: that no dispensation can be granted validly in territory where the civil law would permit opposition to the fulfillment of the promises. But Jombart argues that the very severity itself of such an interpretation argues against its acceptance, for such rigor would surpass all prior austerity in the matter. Jombart favors the more benign interpretation that even where such conditions exist, the dispensing authority can validly grant such dispensations if he has moral certainty of the fulfillment of the promises.

The respected authority, Maroto, seems to be mistakenly relied upon by the *Irish Ecclesiastical Record,* for his analysis seems clearly to the contrary.[182] Maroto holds, first, in that territory in which *perversae leges* exist, which exclude *omnino quamlibet formam cautionem in foro civili iuridice validam*—that the decree renders void any dispensation granted in the face of such affirmative hostile laws. Maroto holds, secondly, that in that territory where the law gives legal effect to the promises, as made in a set mode and form prescribed by the law—the decree renders any dispensation granted in a mode or form contrary to the prescribed legal mode and form. Maroto suggests that in the former territory where positive hostile laws exist, or in the latter situation where it would be impossible to comply with the legal formalities in some particular cases—that recourse should be had to the Holy See.

In conclusion it seems that the better opinion is that of Gasparri and the weight of canonical authority. It must be

[181] *Nouv. Rev. Theol.*, Vol. LXIV (1932), 363.

[182] P. Maroto, *Apollinaris*, Vol. V (1932), p. 5 ff. See n. 6, 7; pp. 9, 10.

remembered that if the severer view is taken no valid dispensations can be granted by the Ordinaries in all of the territory of the United States, England, Ireland, Scotland, Canada and Australia with their millions of Catholic souls and the number of mixed marriages, which seem to be increasing in spite of the ancient attitude of the Church and the modern campaign against the mixed marriage evil.

The legal effects of ante-nuptial promises in any diocese in the United States will be governed by the law of the state in which the diocese is situated. For the jurisdiction in such a matter rests with the individual state rather than with the Federal government. Whether such agreement is enforceable or not will be decided in each state by judicial precedent or by legislative enactment.

In the United States there are no statutes covering the agreement as such. No statute in any jurisdiction directly forbids and there is only one statute which might be construed as tending to uphold such agreements. The legal effect of the promises will be determined by the common law of contracts and the principles of equity which may apply to this form of agreement.

The influence of civil law in this regard suggests the advisability of an enquiry into the present legal status of ante-nuptial promises given in mixed marriages. The promise in the *cautiones* that all children of such marriages shall be baptized and educated in the Roman Catholic faith is of particular importance. The promises must be regularly reduced to writing.[188] No particular form is prescribed and dioceses have differed very widely in the language used to fulfill the canonical requirements.

Such an enquiry shows the need of a form of ante-nuptial agreement that will avoid all ambiguity and meet the essential requirements of the civil law of contracts. Of equal importance is the need of understanding and appreciating the legal reasoning underlying the agreement, which would be of great

[188] Canon 1061, § 2.

benefit in preparing and presenting cases in court proceedings to secure the enforcement of those ante-nuptial promises. With such needs in mind it will be useful to submit an analysis of ante-nuptial agreements from the legal viewpoint, of legal precedents dealing with such promises, and of the true nature of the rights and remedies which may aid in preparing and in presenting cases arising in the future. A form of ante-nuptial agreement is finally suggested as suitable not only to express the will of the parties but also to fulfill the requirements of the civil law of contracts.[184]

[184] See *infra*, Chapter VII.

CHAPTER II

The Apparent Barrier of Legal Precedent

At the outset of any enquiry into the legal status of the ante-nuptial agreement, an objection will be raised at once in some quarters that legal precedent has already decided against the enforceability of such promises. This line of argument would assert that under our Common Law system courts are bound to follow precedent in the form of prior judicial decisions concerning the same legal question. And that argument would proceed further and claim that many such decisions now stand collectively as a barrier to the future recognition or enforcement of ante-nuptial promises. Such an argument can be met squarely without any apprehension. The accumulation of so-called precedents in the form of court decisions deserves some critical analysis and appraisal; but it is submitted that after study they will fail to justify the broad conclusions drawn from them. The barrier will be found to be apparent rather than real. It is necessary to examine the English cases with some care; for the American courts, in considering ante-nuptial promises, have fallen into an undiscriminating citation of an English authority to justify some particular disposition of the case under consideration.[1]

A. THE ENGLISH CASES

From the religious strife in England drastic laws emerged against Catholics that went so far as to make the conducting of a school by a Catholic or assuming the religious education of a child a crime punishable with life imprisonment.[2] And

[1] L. M. Friedman, "The Parental Right to Control the Religious Education of a Child," 29 *Harv. L. Rev.*, 485, 498 (1916).

[2] 11, 12, Wm. III, c. 4.

courts did not hesitate to deprive even parents of custody of their own children, if it seemed likely that the children might not be brought up in the Protestant religion [3] or that a surviving parent contemplated marriage with a Catholic.[4] Though Blackstone cautioned his foreign readers in 1765 that these laws were seldom exerted to their utmost rigor, they still remained a part of the statutory law of England.[5] The statement of Lord Eldon that the court would refrain from interfering with parents in the education of children at that time, 1827,[6] in circumstances in which courts of an earlier date would have taken action to make effective the laws against Catholicism, marks an historic break from earlier precedent. Even as late as 1873 the English Court of Chancery Appeals refers, in a leading case,[7] to the then existing statute of

> 12 Car 2, Ch. 24, 58 which incapacitates a Popish recusant from being appointed a testamentary guardian and which is not repealed by the Geo 4, c 7, or the 26 & 27 Vict c 125.

In the presence of such penal laws and the resulting hostile atmosphere nurtured by contemporary literature, no Catholic dared to invoke the aid of the courts to secure any right to control the religious education of his child.[8]

The development of legal doctrine relating to ante-nuptial promises occurred principally in the period 1852 to 1878. In 1852 a high court stated that it was not aware of any prior case seeking to enforce the agreement; [9] and, in 1878, the Vice-Chancellor emphatically stated that the law had become

[3] 11 & 12 Wm. III, c. 4, sec. 7 (1699).

[4] Edwards *v.* Wise, Barnard, Ch. 139 (1740).

[5] Blackstone, Comm. Book IV, c. 4, p. 57.

[6] Welleslay *v.* Beaufort, 2 Russ 1, 22 (1827).

[7] Andrews *v.* Salt, 8 Law Rep. Chancery App., 622 (1873).

[8] An examination of the appellate cases up to that date reveals no adjudicated case.

[9] *In re* Browne, A Minor, Rolls 2 Ir. Ch. Rep., 151, 162 (1852).

" thoroughly settled " upon the question — the promises were not enforceable.[10] All cases since then have been but an accumulation built upon the cases decided in those years and resting chiefly upon the leading case of Andrews *v.* Salt, decided in 1873.[11] The first landmark of judicial consideration of the ante-nuptial agreement was In re Browne, 1852, an Irish Chancery proceeding. After hearing the evidence the court found as a fact that the existence of such an agreement had not been proved, and rested its decision on this vital point, saying expressly that there was NO WRITTEN OR SATISFACTORY EVIDENCE OF THE EXACT TERMS OF THE CONTRACT.

This, of course, concluded the court's function in this respect. But the court proceeded to examine the novel question and to deliver an elaborate dictum. Though such language is not valid as binding precedent, it was frequently repeated and has found its way down through the reports since that date. The court said that it was aware of the custom of such stipulations but enumerated the difficulties in enforcing them such as the problem of determining custody. Great emphasis was placed upon the difficulty of sequestering funds or property with which to secure such religious training. This can hardly be said to be a practical difficulty today. But, strangely enough, later courts have seized upon this objection and repeated it as a gem of judicial wisdom. And finally in this case the court, still speaking obiter, concluded that enforcement would be detrimental to the interests of the public, although it felt that such a solemn agreement should bind the conscience, saying:

> A large portion of natural equity is left to be administered *in foro conscientiae,* because in addition to the difficulty of propounding precise rules applicable to all cases, a greater detriment and inconvenience would probably ensue from attempting to enforce it in the Courts of Justice, than from leaving it to the decision of the

[10] *In re* Agar-Ellis, 10 Ch. Div., 49, 75 (1878).

[11] Andrews *v.* Salt, 8 L. R. Ch. App., 622 (1873).

power of conscience, and to the various motives by which mankind are ordinarily influenced.[12]

The case of Hill *v.* Hill,[13] which followed ten years later, has also been frequently cited as authority against the enforceability of such promises.

This was a petition by relatives of a deceased Catholic father against his widow who was a Protestant, seeking control of the religious education of a minor daughter. An ante-nuptial agreement was alleged under which the boys were to be educated as Catholics and the girls as Protestants.

After hearing the evidence, Lord Hatherly made his finding that it FAILED TO PROVE THE EXISTENCE OF AN AGREEMENT. It is significant to note in this opinion a dictum in favor of the legal enforceability of the ante-nuptial agreement. This is particularly important; for in subsequent discussion, earlier dicta which are favorable have been overlooked in about the same degree as unfavorable dicta have been paraded as binding precedent. Lord Hatherly said in Hill *v.* Hill that if the parties to the marriage

> enter into an arrangement of that kind which is founded on honor and justice, I confess that I am unable to see any principle on which this court would not give effect to it.

And this statement was approved by the Vice-Chancellor, Sir R. Malins in the later celebrated case of Andrews *v.* Salt.

This brings us to a consideration of that so-called leading case,[14] which has been frequently cited by courts in the United States as well as in England, and which has been quoted often as the legal authority for the proposition that the promises are not legally enforceable. This case should stand as a notable example of judicial error. Cited often as a controlling precedent, it is in fact no precedent at all.

[12] *In re* Browne, A Minor, 2 Ir. Ch. Rep., 151, 160.

[13] Hill *v.* Hill, 40 L. J. Rep. (Eng.), 505 (31 N. S.) (1862).

[14] Andrews *v.* Salt, 8 Law Rep. Chancery App., 622 (1873).

In legal history the blind following of this case as a decisive precedent displays an utter failure to analyze critically and appraise the FACTS and the significance of a supposedly controlling authority.

The circumstances in that interesting case were: A Catholic man promised before marriage that the *girls* born of the marriage would be brought up Protestants, and the Protestant wife promised that the boys would be brought up Catholics. In this important respect, namely different religions for the boys and the girls, that agreement differs from the present-day agreement considered in this analysis. The case concerned a daughter. Because of ill health the father went to his mother's home in another town where he remained until his death. He had sent his wife to her mother's home. There the daughter was born and remained until the time of the proceedings eleven years later. The child was baptized and brought up in the Protestant religion, which was *in accord with the agreement.* The father died before the child was a year old. He left a will naming his brother as testamentary guardian and directing that the children be brought up in the Catholic religion. The guardian allowed nine years to pass before bringing court proceedings to enforce the provisions of the father's will. For all of that time, except three months, the child had lived with the maternal grandmother and been educated in the Protestant religion. Finally proceedings were brought which amounted to an attempt to repudiate the agreement; for *the promise was to bring the girls up as Protestants.*

The decision was against the guardian and supported the ante-nuptial agreement. And the court expressly based its finding upon the agreement, the fact that the father had allowed the daughter to be baptized and brought up a Protestant, and the lapse of time before the testamentary guardian attempted to enforce his rights. In the course of the opinion the Vice-Chancellor reviewed the earlier case of Hill *v.* Hill and remarked that Lord Hatherly, the judge in that case said:

if he had come to the conclusion that there was such an arrangement he would have attached importance to it; not, indeed, on the question whether there was an abjuration of *all* duties to the child, . . . Therefore I cannot see that there is any abjuration whatever of the duty of a parent in agreeing that, instead of being brought up in that particular form of Christianity to which he himself belongs, the child should, in deference to the feelings of the mother, be brought up in her particular form of the Christian religion. Therefore I entirely agree with what I take to be Lord *Hatherly's* opinion, that if such an agreement as that is established, it is one to which this court would feel every indication to give effect.[15]

An appeal was taken and the appellate court affirmed the Vice-Chancellor and made several additional findings of fact which support the decision; viz., that the child would be dependent upon charity for her support, that those to whom she had been entrusted were willing to continue that support and a separation from her present surroundings could not be made " without prejudice to her happiness, her prospects in life and possibly her health." The Court of Appeals found as the lower court had that the deceased had not only promised his wife that the girls should be educated as Protestants, but also had practically carried out that promise without objection until the daughter was nearly nine years old. The original order and decree affirming it was, of course, the only legal way of determining the matter. The ante-nuptial decree was supported expressly by the Vice-Chancellor and in effect by the Court of Appeal. The counsel for the Protestant grandmother had so many valid arguments in her favor that he did not stress the ante-nuptial agreement in the appeal. He waived its importance, saying expressly that

It is of no importance whether the ante-nuptial contract could be enforced as a legal contract or not. . . . The real question is the happiness and interest of the child.[16]

[15] Andrews *v.* Salt, 8 Law Rep. Ch. App., 622, 628 (note) (1873). (Italics "all" inserted.)

[16] Andrews *v.* Salt, *supra*, p. 634.

The court, however, though deciding that the child should be brought up as the father had promised in the ante-nuptial agreement, and though the counsel had not pressed that agreement in argument, proceeded to consider the effect of such an agreement. And from such consideration came the famous passage which has been so often quoted ever since:

The first question we shall consider is, what is the legal effect of an agreement made before marriage between a husband and wife of different religious persuasions that boys should be educated in the religion of the father, and girls in the religion of the mother? We are of the opinion that such an agreement is not binding as a legal contract. No damages can be recovered for a breach of it in a Court of Law and it cannot be enforced by a suit for specific performance in equity. We think that a father cannot bind himself conclusively by contract to exercise, in all events, in a particular way, rights which the law gives him for the benefit of his children, and not for his own. We entirely agree with the decision of the Lord Chancellor of Ireland (*In re* Meades (1)), in which he held that the court could not during the lifetime of a father compel him out of his own funds to educate a child in a different religion from his own. So, also, if after a father's death it appeared to the Court that it was most for the benefit of a child to be educated in the religion of his father, we think that the Court would not abstain from ordering him to be so educated because the father had agreed with the mother that the child should be educated in her religion. On the other hand, if, after the death of the father, circumstances happen, which in the opinion of the Court, make it for the benefit of a child to be educated in the religion of the mother, and the question arises whether the father had so acted that he ought to be held in this Court to have waived or abandoned his right to have his child educated in his own religion, the fact that the father before marriage promised the mother that the girls, the issue of the marriage, should be educated in her religion, is a circumstance to which in our opinion weight, and perhaps great weight, ought to be attached. This appears to have been the opinion of Lord Hatherly, from what he said on the subject in Hill *v.* Hill (1), though in that case he did not think that the fact of the agreement having been made was satisfactorily proved.[17]

In 1878, five years after this case had been decided, the same Vice-Chancellor Malins was confronted with the perplexing question again.[18] A Protestant had orally promised his Catholic wife-to-be that all children should be brought up in the Catholic religion. The first child was baptized a Catholic against the wishes of the father. The religious discord continued until the father brought a petition to have the children made wards of the court and to have directions made covering their religious education. The mother filed a counter petition to have the children educated as Catholics.

Previously, in Andrews *v.* Salt, Sir Malins had said that he could see no principle of law in opposition to enforcing the ante-nuptial promises. There he had said that he "entirely agreed" with Lord Hatherly's judgment that if such an agreement was proved to exist, "it is one to which this court would feel every inclination to give effect."[19] But now his attitude was entirely different. The agreement no longer is persuasive, and a father's promise to bring the children up in a religion other than his own is "*thoroughly settled not to be binding.*" Citing In re Browne, he then refers to the situation where a father permitted a child to be brought up in another religion until the child was old enough to be capable of entertaining particular religious views, and adds: "*That was the ground on which I refused to interfere and on which* the Court of Appeals *refused to interfere in Andrews* v. *Salt.*" And he concluded that Andrews *v.* Salt was "the latest authority on this subject." No new case had arisen. In view of the scanty amount of judicial precedent it is certainly fair to ask, when and how did it become *thoroughly* settled that the promise was not

[17] James L. in Andrews *v.* Salt, 8 Law Rep. Ch. App. Cases, pp. 635, 636, 637 (1873).

[18] *In re* Agar-Ellis, 10 Ch. Div., 49 (1878).

[19] Andrews *v.* Salt, *supra*, p. 628.

binding? Five years before, the Vice-Chancellor had described the arrangement as one "founded on honor *and justice.*" Now, completely ignoring that opinion, he expresses sorrow and regret that the wife

> has set at defiance the authority of the father over the children . . . seeming to have entirely forgotten that by the laws of *England*, by the laws of Christianity, and by the Constitution of society, when there is a difference between husband and wife, it is the duty of the wife to submit to the husband.[20]

It is apparent that the Chancellor had entirely overlooked the fact that she had married under that express stipulation. And likewise, he had forgotten his own agreement with Lord Hatherly that the court would feel every inclination to give effect to such an agreement and knew of no principle or law which would preclude such aid. But if the Vice-Chancellor was embarrassed he turned his friendly glance toward Ireland and was relieved to find that Lord O'Hagan, who the Vice-Chancellor is careful to tell us is "a Roman Catholic as we all know," had given a decision against the enforceability of the agreement. In that case a Protestant had made the agreement before marrying a Catholic woman. She died, leaving two children eleven and eight years old. The father had his wife's sister come into the home, agreeing to have her continue their Catholic training. Contemplating another marriage, he changed his attitude and insisted on the children now becoming Protestants. It is to be noted that the mother had died. The ensuing controversy resulted in a petition by the aunt against the father, asking that the children be made wards of the aunt, and that the father be restrained from interfering with the Catholic training. Lord O'Hagan refused to interfere with the father, though he intimated a different result would have been possible if the remedy had been sought earlier, and had he found that the children had acquired a settled Catholic

[20] *In re* Agar-Ellis, 10 Law Rep. Chanc. Div. 49, p. 55 (1878).

religious belief. This very interesting opinion begins in this fashion:

The authority of a father to guide and govern the education of his child is a very sacred thing, bestowed by the Almighty and to be sustained to the uttermost by human law. It is not to be abrogated or abridged, without the most coercive reason. For the parent and the child alike, its maintenance is essential, that their reciprocal relations may be fruitful of happiness and virtue; and no disrupting intervention should be allowed between them, whilst those relations are pure and wholesome and conducive to their mutual benefit.[21]

A grandiloquent paragraph it is—but beside the question! Had the father not abridged his right by the agreement? Exaltation of paternal power even leads the jurist into the lyrical and poetic passage:

Morning, noon, and night—month after month—they are subjected to the influence of a father to whom they are unquestionably devoted; and as

" Our nature is subdued
To what it works in, like the dyer's hand." [22]

Finally, after much elaboration, he wistfully concludes:

I do not know what may be the future of these little ones, whether as the palimpsest often shows freshly the original inscription after it has been long concealed, the impressions communicated at the mother's knee may not find development hereafter, or whether those by which they have covered and subdued may not forever forbid their re-appearance, no one can tell with any confidence.[23]

Swayed by Lord O'Hagan's reasoning, Vice-Chancellor Malins departed from his former opinion that the ante-nuptial arrangement, founded on honor and justice, should be and

[21] *In re* Meades, Minors, 5 Ir. R. Eq., 98, 103 (1871).

[22] *In re* Meades, Minors, 5 Ir. R. Eq., 98, 100 (1871).

[23] *Ibidem*, pp. 117-118.

would be enforced by the law. The Court of Appeal affirmed the decision but expressly stated that the "ground on which we base our decision on the main subject viz. — *the power and jurisdiction of the father.*"[24] The hostile atmosphere towards the Catholic religion, however, is felt in the opinion of James L. J. in these passages:

> The mother conceived herself to be warranted in disregarding her husband's express and positive wishes and commands as to the religious education of her daughters, and availed herself of all the opportunities afforded by the relations between a mother and daughters, who had never been separated, not only to impress their minds with the great cardinal truths and the religious and moral duties common to both modes of faith, but to instruct and indoctrinate them, so far as they were capable of receiving them, with the peculiar tenets constituting the characteristic difference of her own Church, and to accustom them, as a matter of religious duty, to the performance of certain religious acts, the practical expression of those peculiar tenets, such as the adoration of the Virgin, the invocation of patron saints, and the practice of confession. . . . And, being of opinion that the father has retained his right to direct the religious education of his children, and the father being minded that they should not be taken to mass, confession, or the like, the causing or permitting them to be so taken, in direct disobedience to the father's commands, is a wrong to them as well as to him.[25]

The doctrine of Andrews *v.* Salt was now seemingly entrenched in English law. To take successive cases of so-called precedents and to add a detailed analysis of each would lengthen this consideration unnecessarily. The reasoning of the decisions in cases cited now in England and also in the United States against the enforceability of ante-nuptial promises reveals a striking absence of relevancy in nearly all

[24] Agar *v.* Lascelles, 10 Law Rep. Chanc. Div. 49, 76 (1878). (Italics inserted.)

[25] Agar-Ellis *v.* Lascelles, 10 Law Rep. Chanc. Div. 49, 70, 75 (1878).

the cases. Several have the feature, common to some of the cases cited above, that no ante-nuptial agreement existed between the parties.[26]

In another case, the court found that the agreement was not made before marriage.[27]

Another court questioned whether the agreement before it was a contract between the parties or an agreement with the

[26] Stourton *v.* Stourton, 8 De. G. M. & G., 760 (1857). This is another early case which is frequently cited. Both parents of the child were Catholics at the time of marriage. Consequently there was *not any ante-nuptial agreement.* The father had died and the mother had become a Protestant. The relatives of the Catholic father delayed five years while the boy, a lad of ten, followed his mother in becoming a Protestant. The court interviewed the lad and found that he seemed to have had "more minute and close instruction as a Protestant, upon some at least of the main points of difference between the Church of England and that of Rome, than is usual in England with boys of his age" (and concludes) "that the child's tranquillity and health, his temporal happiness, and, if that can exist apart from spiritual welfare, his spiritual welfare also, are too likely now to suffer importantly from an endeavor at effacing his Protestant impressions, not to render such attempt unsafe and improper."

It may be remarked in passing that such language points to our later claim in this paper that religious belief and human happiness are so interwoven that the right of *the Catholic party acquired by the agreement* to control the religious education may fairly be said to be a right of personality, and further that baptism and early religious training is important in fixing religious status.

Hawksworth *v.* Hawksworth, Law Rep., 6 Chancery App., 539 (1871).

A Catholic man married a Protestant. *They did not enter into an ante-nuptial agreement.* He died leaving a widow and an infant daughter six months old. Eight years later in a suit instituted for the administration of the deceased's estate the court made an order that the child should be brought up in the religion of her father and refused to interview the child. The court felt that the principle of Stourton *v.* Stourton (*supra*) in examining the child to see whether it had acquired distinct and fixed religious views should be limited.

[27] D'Alton *v.* D'Alton, Law Reports, 4 Prob. Div., 87 (1878). The agreement was made several years after marriage and in consideration of the wife granting a reconciliation to her husband, who had been living in adultery. The child was placed in the custody of a third party on the ground that it was for the best welfare of the child.

Church.[28] But it added that it was clear law that such an agreement was not binding upon the authority of Andrews *v.* Salt. It neglected its own duty to determine whether an agreement existed, before discussing its legal effect. Curiously the court repeats Lord O'Hagan's classic difficulty with such agreements in compelling a father to educate, out of his own funds, a child in a religion different from his own.

In other cases the court decided that the Catholic party had lost whatever rights he had by laches—the failure to assert rights over a long period of time such as nine years in one case; [29] or had lost his rights by misconduct.[30] In other cases the court decided that any rights under the agreement were waived by the party permitting the child to be "openly introduced to a communion directly opposed" to his parent's alleged religious belief.[31] And, in another case, the court found that the petitioner was a "nominal Catholic" who had allowed his child to be brought up in another religion until it had acquired contrary settled religious convictions.[32] Thus *it can be readily understood and appreciated that* English precedents lose heavily when subjected to legal criticism rather than mechanical approval. What remain can be further reduced by the elimination of those cases which rest upon the doctrine, no longer law, of the father's supreme right in the family domain.[33] It is a doctrine largely changed now by statute and

[28] *In re* Nevin, 2 Law Rep. Ch., 299 (1891). The temper of this opinion can be seen in the remarks of *Kay, L. J.*, that the promises were not "as I think by reason of any agreement between themselves, but in consequence of a rule of the Romish Church" (p. 315), and of *Lindley, L. F.*, "whether it is to be regarded as a contract between the husband and wife I do not know—it rather looks like a condition imposed by a higher power" (p. 311).

[29] Stourton *v.* Stourton, *supra.*

[30] D'Alton *v.* D'Alton, Law Reports & Prob. Div., 87 (1778). *In re* Newton, 1 Ch. 740 (1896).

[31] Hill *v.* Hill, Law Jour. 40, N. S., Vol. 31, pp. 505, 512 (1862).

[32] *In re* Ward, 2 Irish Reports, K. B. Div., 19, 32 (1924).

[33] It will be noted that some of these cases have already been considered in this study.

decision. But in these cases it had far-reaching effect, often controlling the decision and affecting the consideration in nearly every case. Such extreme language as characterized the decisions seems strange today. The courts called the father's right "an absolute right," which is not to be "abrogated or abridged without the most coercive reason." [34] It is an undoubted right "as master in his own house, as king and ruler" and a right that has been supported "by every case in this court." [35] The child is not to be removed from his custody even where the father is living in adultery,[36] and the father's right of control persists even after death.[37] The father's right to control the religious education was not affected by the liberalizing Guardianship of Infants Act of 1886.[38] This preponderant legal power of the father in matters of custody and religious training has been reduced drastically by the late English statute of 1925, Ch. 4, Sect. 1, as follows:

> Where in any proceeding before any court (whether or not a court with the meaning of the Guardianship of Infants Act (1886) the custody or upbringing of an infant . . . is in question . . . the court in deciding the question shall regard the welfare of the infant as the first and foremost consideration and shall not take into consideration whether from any other point of view the claim of the father, or any right at common law possessed by the father in respect of such custody, upbringing . . . is superior to that of the mother, or the claim of the mother is superior to that of the father.

[34] *In re* Scanlon, 40 Law Rep. (Ch. Div.), 200 (1889). *In re* Gray, 2 Ir. Rep. K. B. Div. 684, 687 (1902).

[35] *In re* Meades, 5 Ir. R. Eq. 98 (1870). *In re* Agar-Ellis, 10 Ch. Div. 49, 75 (1878).

[36] Malins, V. C., *In re* Agar-Ellis, 10 Ch. Div. 49, 57 (1878).

[37] Lord O'Hagan, *In re* Meades, Minors, 5 Ir. R. Eq. 98 (1871), quoting Ball *v.* Ball, 2 Sim., 35 (1857).

[38] Stourton *v.* Stourton, 8 De G. M. & G. 760 (1857). Davis *v.* Davis, 26 J. P. 260 (1862). Hill *v.* Hill, 40 L. J. Rep. 505 (31 N. S.) (1862). Hawksworth *v.* Hawksworth, Law Rep., 6 Ch. App. 539 (1871), p. 19.

This is of great importance in our present consideration, because the great stress laid upon the father's former extreme right may fairly be said to have been a determining factor in shaping precedent in practically all of those cases.[39] The modern courts find no great difficulty in determining that the father may lose his right.[40]

The words in which judge after judge refers to what I thus call the loss of his right to dictate the religious education of his children are almost bewildering in their variety—He may " lose " it; he may " abandon " it; he may " forfeit " it; he may " abdicate " it; he may by his conduct " disable " himself from making an application to the Court. He may " disentitle " himself. He may place himself in such a position as to render it not merely better for the children, but essential to their safety or welfare in some very serious and important respect, that his rights should be treated as lost or suspended—should be superseded or interfered with.[41]

Before drawing final conclusions from this review of the English authorities, it is well worth while to pause and, having in mind the present tendency to enforce rights of personality, to see running through the cases a strand of judicial feeling that the agreement should be enforced in justice to the Catholic party, if the court were unhampered by precedent and practical difficulties. This feeling is illustrated by the following extracts from opinions:

An ante-nuptial agreement is one which he may consider himself bound in honor to carry out but it is not legally binding.[42]

The Vice-Chancellor said:

Therefore I entirely agree with what I take to be Lord Hatherly's

[39] *In re* Scanlon, 40 Law Rep., Ch. Div., 200 (1889). *In re* Story, Ir. Rep., Vol. 2, p. 328 (1916).

[40] Davis *v.* Davis, 26 J. P. 260 (1862). Hill *v.* Hill, 40 L. J. Rep. 505 (31 N. S.) (1862).

[41] Dodd, J., *In re* Story, 2 Ir. Rep. K. B. Div. 328, 351 (1916).

[42] Bowen, L. J., *In re* Nevin, 2 Law Rep. Chanc. 299, 313 (1891).

opinion, that if such an agreement as that is established it is one to which this Court would feel every inclination to give effect.[43]

In a later decision in Scotland the court, in effect, carried out the agreement made by a Protestant woman with a Catholic husband, but expressly rested its decision upon the father's superior right. Speaking of the mother's (respondent's) promise, that the children should be brought up as Catholics, one of the judges said:

Now, I think that, giving a fair construction to the undertaking which was signed by the respondent in this case, that meant that the education of these children should be continued to be given by that denomination. And accordingly, upon that ground I take the view that the position of the respondent is not justified.[44]

The possibility of the father's preponderant right yielding was referred to by another judge in the same decision.

The view which has been taken by the Courts, both in this country and in England, is, I think, both just and expedient, viz., that prima facie it is in the interests of a child that he should be educated in the religion of his parents, or, if there be a difference between the religion of the father and of the mother, in the religion of the father. This rule is very far from being a universal one, and in certain familiar classes of circumstances it has to yield to other considerations.[45]

And the agreement may be

" a circumstance to which weight, and perhaps great weight will be given " in the language of an English court.[46]
And the question arises whether the father so acted that he ought to be held in this court to have waived or abandoned his right to have

[43] Andrews *v.* Salt, L. R. 8 Ch. App. 622, p. 628 (1873).

[44] Lord Mackenzie, one of the judges in O'Donnell *v.* O'Donnell, 1918, Scotch case, 14, 19.

[45] Lord Skerrington, in O'Donnell *v.* O'Donnell (*supra*).

[46] *In re* Clark, 21 Ch. Div., 817, 824 (1882).

his child educated in his own religion. The fact that the father before marriage promised the mother that girls, the issue of the marriage, should be educated in her religion, *is a circumstance to which, in our opinion, weight, and perhaps great weight, ought to be attached.*[47]

The language of Lord O'Hagan was adopted verbatim by the Vice-Chancellor in an English case:

and one can hardly avoid a feeling of natural regret that an engagement so solemn, so openly avowed, so strengthened by repetition, so confirmed by the consecration of the grave, should have been disregarded.[48]

It can be seen from this brief analysis that many English cases are not valid precedents against the enforceability of ante-nuptial promises. The body of supposedly contrary precedent is strikingly reduced by the elimination of those cases in which the court *failed to find that an ante-nuptial agreement existed.* From the remainder it is fair to exclude all those *which were decided on grounds other than the agreement,* such as the misconduct of the Catholic party or his open waiver of rights acquired through the agreement. And the balance can finally be reduced to the minimum by the elimination of those which rest upon the now obsolete doctrine that a father is absolute " king and ruler " possessed of an inalienable right to control the religious upbringing of the children. So diminished is the body of the precedent after these legitimate deductions that only one English case decided by a high court stands out, in which the agreement was contested during the life time of the parties and repudiated by the courts.[49] And this case Agar-Ellis depends upon Andrews *v.* Salt, a mistaken precedent, and upon *In re* Meades, the Irish phantasy of " father power " by Lord O'Hagan.[50]

[47] Lord O'Hagan, in *In re* Meades, 5 Ir. R. Eq. 98 (1873). (Italics inserted.)

[48] *In re* Agar-Ellis, 10 Ch. Div. 49, p. 58 (1878).

[49] *In re* Agar-Ellis, 10 Ch. Div. 49, p. 58 (1878).

[50] *In re* Meades, 5 Ir. R. Eq. 98 (1873).

B. THE AMERICAN CASES

As has been said earlier, the American courts have cited without discrimination the supposed English precedents, and they have erred seriously in the use of American precedents as well. For, in citing the latter, courts have cited many cases as precedents against the enforceability of the promises, in which the parent was unmarried,[51] one or both parents were dead,[52] a statute controlled the decision,[53] or the court was without jurisdiction to pass on the question.[54]

The Supreme Court of the United States has not passed upon the question of the legal enforceability of the ante-nuptial promises; nor have the Supreme Courts of most of the states, including the more populous states of New York, Illinois, Massachusetts and California. The other courts which have considered the matter have often been lower courts. They have carefully avoided the religious question and rested the decision upon any other possible ground. Not one case is reported in which a supreme court considered the enforceability of the promises during the life-time of the parents.

All of the American courts that have considered the ante-nuptial agreement have weighted down their decisions with heavy citations of those English cases, which we have previously discussed. It is apparent that several of the American courts, when citing English cases, have either not read the actual decisions, or totally failed to appraise their legal value. And it may be said at this point that the propriety of such citation may be seriously questioned. To be sure, the common law of England does stand in some degree as valid precedent for American courts. But that use has distinct limitations, parti-

[51] Purinton *v.* Jamrock, 195 Mass., 187; 80 N. E., 802 (1907).

[52] *In re* Lamb's Estate, 139 N. Y. Supp., 685 (1912).

[53] *In re* Laura Doyle, 16 Mo. App., 159 (1884).

[54] Brewer *v.* Cary, 148 Mo. App., 193; 127 S. W., 685 (1910).

cularly where religious matters are the subject of the proceedings. As one New York court has said:

> This is a land where all forms of religion are both free and protected, and where the rights of fathers, within the law, are still recognized and enforced in proper cases. . . . These are tremendous differences, and thus it is that the common law of the people of this state and that of the people of modern England are very often very far apart in principle and application.[55]

Are such English decisions as we have considered, made at a time closely following a long period of Catholic persecution, when some disabling statutes still remained in force, and given in a place where state religion opposed Catholicism, still valid precedents in United States courts? Can they properly be applied in the full vigor of their anti-Catholic tenor in a country such as ours committed to the principle of religious equality and the denial of a state Church? American courts have not paused to think about this and have rushed headlong into a promiscuous citation of English cases. In considering these cases, it is convenient to limit our immediate enquiry to the few American cases most often cited. We shall take up the others in a subsequent chapter dealing with cases arising after the death of one or both parents and involving the added question of award of custody. They form a separate group and have been decided frequently by reference to a particular statute.

The American case cited most frequently against the enforceability of ante-nuptial agreements is Brewer *v.* Cary,[56] a Missouri case. A Catholic woman married a Protestant who made the ante-nuptial promises. Three children were born to the couple. The Catholic mother died. Her father, who had been god-father as well to one of the children, brought a bill in equity against the father, who had determined to bring up

[55] *In re* Lamb's Estate, 139 N. Y. Supp., 685 (1912).

[56] Brewer *v.* Cary, 148 Mo. App., 193; 127 S. W., 685 (1910).

the children Protestants. The petition asked that the other children be baptized and that all be brought up in the Catholic religion. The father demurred on three grounds: (1) *that the court did not have jurisdiction of the action;* (2) that the complainant, as god-father or as grand-father, did not have a legal standing in court as complainant in the action; (3) that the facts alleged did not constitute a sufficient basis for legal action. A demurrer in law is equivalent to an admission of the facts alleged, solely however for purpose of argument, and a challenge to their sufficiency as a matter of law in stating a legal cause of action. A demurrer to the jurisdiction of the court strikes directly at the very right of the court itself to consider and to adjudicate the matter in question. Jurisdiction is the very first and fundamental requirement for the validity of a court's decree. To give judicial proceedings any validity, there must be a competent tribunal.[57] That is elementary. Hence, it is clear that the first objection "*that the court did not have jurisdiction of the action*" was fundamental. If the court did not have such jurisdiction, and so decided, then the matter was terminated. *And the court decided precisely that.* Viz,: it did not have jurisdiction. But, instead of stopping there, the court proceeded to deliver an opinion which clearly falls outside the definition of controlling legal precedent and into the broad remainder *of legal opinions called dicta.*

The opinion of the court is binding precedent only so far as it expresses the statement of law *necessarily* involved in deciding the particular proceeding before it.[58] So far as the opinion goes beyond a statement of the proposition of law necessarily involved in the case, the words contained in the opinion, whether they be right or wrong, are merely words spoken, *dicta.* No *dictum* is authority of the highest sort. To give it such weight would be to give judges power to decide

[57] Pennoyer *v.* Neff, 95 U. S., 714 (1877).

[58] Boggs *v.* Waun, 58 Fed., 681 (1893) (U. S. D. C.).

in advance a case not before them for adjudication, a merely hypothetical case, and to bind by their opinion the court before which that hypothetical case may eventually become an actual proceeding.[59] The Federal Court in an opinion of a Circuit Court of Appeals has expressed the accepted meaning in the following passage:

A dictum is defined to be " an opinion expressed by the court which, not being necessarily involved in the case, lacks the force of an adjudication." The Supreme Court of the United States has held that, in order to make an opinion a decision, there must have been an application of the judicial mind to the precise question necessary to be determined to fix the rights of the parties; and, therefore, said the learned judge delivering this opinion, " this court has never held itself bound by any part of an opinion which was not needful to the ascertainment of the question between the parties." [60] The writer has emphasized this difference between opinion which is valid precedent and opinion which is merely dicta, because of its importance in appraising the value of this decision in Brewer *v.* Cary. To repeat, in its opinion the court in this case had decided that it did not have jurisdiction. Whatever it said beyond that finding would clearly lack the prestige of established precedent controlling the determination of future proceedings and would be entitled only to the deference which is given to a judge's opinion.[61] In brief conclusion, referring to the ante-nuptial promise to rear the children in the Catholic faith, the court expressed a vigorous opinion that the contract was not enforceable at law or in equity.[62]

In the course of its decision this court referred with approval to the language used in the case of *In re Laura Doyle* decided

[59] See Wambaugh, *The Study of Cases*, pp. 12-14.

[60] *In re* Woodruff, 96 Fed., 317, 322 (1899).

[61] *In re* Woodruff, 96 Fed. 317 (U. S. D. C.) (1899).

[62] Brewer *v.* Cary, 148 Mo. App., 193; 127 S. W., pp. 685, 688 (1910).

by a lower court also in Missouri.[63] And, since this case has also been frequently cited as authority against the legal value of the ante-nuptial promise, it is worth while to examine the facts of this latter case, the decision, and the curious temper of the opinion. It was a petition for a writ of habeas corpus instituted by a Catholic father to secure custody of his child. The child's mother was dead. The father had placed the child in an orphanage, which gave the child to the defendant, a Protestant. No consent for such transfer had been given by the father. The court, of course, granted the father's petition. The facts of the case presented no difficulty. The father's paramount right as parent to custody of the child, and the welfare of the child, were the two determining legal principles governing the decision. But the judge, one Justice Blakewell, delivered a lengthy opinion, irrelevant and characterized by a marked religious bitterness.[64] He said that, in determining custody, the courts decide the matter

> with a view mainly to the child's interest, which we must look upon as altogether paramount to the claims of its father, who is not vested by the law with any absolute right to its custody. . . . In determining what will be best for the child, we cannot under the system of law which we are appointed to administer, look at that (religion). . . . She (the State) looks with equal eye upon all forms of a so-called Christianity and subjects no one to any disability for rejecting Christianity in any form, nor for rejecting the generally accepted doctrines of natural religion. A father in Missouri forfeits no rights to the custody and control of his child by being, or becoming, an atheist. Nor are his rights in this respect increased before the law by his believing rightly. The law does not profess to know what is a right belief.

It requires no astute legal reasoning to discount the legal value of these two decisions. The former was made by a court

[63] 16 Mo. App., 159 (1884).

[64] *In re* Laura Doyle, *ibidem*, p. 166.

which admitted its own lack of jurisdiction; and the latter by a court which based its decision upon totally different grounds, though proceeding in addition to express its religious venom.[65] These two cases, with the earlier English cases, particularly Andrews *v.* Salt, have raised the apparent barrier of precedent in the United States against the legal enforceability of ante-nuptial promises; for these cases have been cited repeatedly to prove that the agreement is not legally binding. The American cases which were decided with reference to statutes will be considered in a later chapter. As in the English cases, it will be seen also in the American cases that scarcely any have occurred during the lifetime of the parents. The question of the legal enforceability has usually arisen in situations where the question of custody was before the court after the death of one or both parents. However a few more cases are reported in which the enforceability of the agreement was considered. An early Pennsylvania court [66] intimated that the ante-nuptial promise would be binding if action had been brought while the Catholic spouse was living. In the actual facts presented to the Court, the Protestant father was dead and the mother insane. The father had been unable to provide for the children, who had been placed in the home of the Protestant grandmother and had been brought up as Protestants. A maternal aunt petitioned for custody several years after the death of the father. The court refused the petition of the Catholic maternal aunt "because of the age of the children, their hitherto religious training and environment, their antipathy to the proceeding"

[65] "To the Protestant, the Catholic religion must be a system of superstition; to the Jew it must be one of imposture; and, to the unbeliever, the old historic religions of the Jew and Catholic, and the various sects of Protestantism, are alike false, and the profession of any of them a confession, so far, of moral or intellectual weakness."—*Ibidem*, p. 167.

"....both the father's and the mother's side are all Catholics—and Irish Catholics—that is to say, Catholics of the very strongest hereditary faith." —*Ibidem*, p. 169.

[66] Comm. *v.* McClelland, 70 Pa. Sup. Ct. 273 (1918).

and the delay of several years by the Catholic aunt in bringing the petition.[67] Several very substantial grounds were relied upon by the court for its decision. However, the court said that it would have decided otherwise and would have granted the petition of the Catholic aunt if the proceeding had been brought while the children were still young, and further, that the ante-nuptial agreement would have been the basis for such decision. The court said:

It is not likely that the father would have raised any objection, and, if he had, his stipulation entered into at the time of his marriage would have been a sufficient answer.

This, of course, has only the value of dictum. The strongest declaration by an American court in favor of the enforceability of the ante-nuptial promises is a dictum of an Ohio court. The parents had entered an ante-nuptial agreement. After the death of the parents, the relatives of the father and mother brought a court proceeding to determine custody. The decree allowed custody to remain with the paternal Protestant uncle. But the court explicitly declared that:

the father indicated the strongest intentions to utterly repudiate the promises that he had made at the marriage altar, and so solemnly subscribed, as a part of the consideration entering into marital relations with Anna Scanlon. . . . As between the parties . . . when the wife was living the binding force and inviolability of this contract would be recognized by all courts, and sanctioned by the moral sense of all mankind, . . . If this controversy . . . was between the father and the mother, a court would utterly fail in its duty not to make this agreement work an estoppel of the father's right to divert the course of religious nurture so provided for. . . . The law gives force to such a compact in dealing with the rights of parents . . . the agreement has binding operation in point of law.[68]

[67] Comm. *v.* McClelland, *ibidem.*

[68] *In re* Luck, 10 Ohio, Dec., p. 1 (1900).

It can easily be seen that there is an absence in American decisions of any body of precedent against the legal enforceability of the agreement. It is only an apparent barrier raised by the careless citation of supposed precedents and oft-repeated dicta. However robust in expression, dicta cannot thus raise themselves by their bootstraps to the elevated rank of controlling precedents. Both English and American cases are of illusory power only. The real paucity of legal decisions is apparent. With pre-judgments based upon such mistaken precedents removed, the courts may proceed to consider the real nature and affect of the ante-nuptial agreement.

CHAPTER III

The Ante-Nuptial Agreement as a Legal Contract

It is submitted that the ante-nuptial agreement, containing as it does the non-Catholic's promise to have the children of the marriage baptized and educated in the Catholic faith, given in exchange for the promise of the Catholic to marry and his or her consequent change of status, fulfills the requirements of a legally binding contract. "Contract" has been variously defined as

a promise, or set of promises, to which the law attaches legal obligation,[1]

or as:

a promise, or a set of promises, for the unexcused non-performance of which the law gives a remedy or the performance of which the law in some way recognizes as a duty.[2]

The law gives legal force and effect to promises of this type of agreement as contrasted with the more formal requirements of contracts under seal. Indeed, in this type of contract, the following conditions alone are necessary; namely, those which show the element of mutual assent and the technical legal consideration as known to the common law: viz., (1) parties of legal capacity; (2) an expression of mutual assent by the

[1] Williston on Contracts, Sect. 1 (1920).

[2] Restatement of the Law of Contracts, American Law Institute, Chap. 1, Sec. 1.

The American Law Institute, composed of legal experts, prominent lawyers and judges in the U. S. has attempted an authoritative restatement of the law. The law of contracts has been recently completed. It is this statement that is relied upon in this text.

parties to a promise or set of promises; (3) a valid technical consideration, and (4) the absence of any subject matter in the agreement, the performance of which would be contrary to public policy.[3] The meaning and significance of this requirement of the presence of consideration and the absence of matter contrary to public policy, and the relation of both requirements to our problem will be discussed presently. As to the first two requirements, no difficulty arises in cases involving ante-nuptial agreements. Difficulty arises, however as to the third; namely, whether the agreement fulfills the requirements of civil law as to the valid consideration, which has been defined as

> Mutual promises in each of which the promisor undertakes some act or forebearance that will be, or apparently may be, detrimental to the promisor or beneficial to the promisee, and neither of which is rendered void by any rule of law other than that relating to consideration.[4]

The legal consequences are not affected, however, by the fact that the consideration consists of one or several promises by one or both parties.[5] The adequacy of marriage itself or of a promise to marry as consideration for another promise is settled beyond all doubt.[6] The great number of contracts having marriage or a promise of marriage for consideration and

[3] Williston, *op. cit.*, Chapt. I, Sect. 1.

[4] Williston, *op. cit.*, Chap. VI, Sect. 103 f.

[5] The Restatement of the Law of Contracts gives the following relevant definition of consideration:

(c) the creation, modification or destruction of a legal relation or
(d) a return promise, bargained for and given in exchange for the promise.
(e) Consideration may be given to the promisor or to some other person. It may be given by the promisee or by some other person.

The Restatement of the Law of Contracts, Sect. 83.

" Consideration is sufficient for as many promises as are bargained for and given in exchange for it, if it would be sufficient consideration for one of them, if that one alone were bargained for . ."

[6] Williston, *op. cit.*, Vol. I, Sec. 486.

difficulties with regard to their proof or disproof resulted at an early date in the enactment in England of a statute which restricted the aid of the courts to those contracts reduced to writing. The statute provided:

that no action shall be brought whereby to charge any person or any agreement made in consideration of marriage, unless the agreement or some memorandum or note thereof shall be in writing, and signed by the party to be charged therewith or some person thereunto by him lawfully authorized. . . .[7]

In the United States this provision has been considered in force by virtue of the general adoption of such of the early English statutes as were adopted to the condition and polity of the country. In most states there has been an express enactment of a similar statute; and in others, in the absence of such enactment, the courts have held that even an oral promise in consideration of marriage is enforceable.[8] Such statutory provisions did not affect the validity of such contracts but rather refused a remedy through the courts enforcing them, unless they were reduced to writing. The proposition, therefore, that marriage is sufficient legal consideration for a contract has been upheld continually by courts and supported by authoritative writers.[9]

Story, J., in a decision of the Supreme Court of the United States, said:

Marriage in contemplation of the law, is not only a valuable consideration to support such a settlement, but is a consideration of the highest value; and from motives of the soundest policy is upheld with a steady resolution. The husband and wife, parties to such a contract, are therefore deemed, in the highest sense, purchasers for a valuable consideration.[10]

[7] 29 Car. II, Chap. III, Secs. 4, 5 (1677).

[8] Lewis *v.* Tapman, 90 Md. 294, 45 A. 459 (1900).

[9] Williston: Contracts I, Sec. 486, p. 936 (1920).

[10] Mangae *v.* Thompson, 7 Peters (U. S.) 389, 393-394 (1833).

Consequently it becomes apparent even to the casual reader that the ante-nuptial agreement contains the essential elements of a legal contract.

Further enquiry leads us to analyze the nature of the claim to rights acquired in such a contract.

CHAPTER IV

The Nature of the Right[1] Acquired in the Ante-Nuptial Agreement

It it thus seen from the statements of the law that the courts of the United States and England have had no difficulty in recognizing the contractual nature of ante-nuptial agreements concerning the conveyances of property or other similar interests and have not questioned their legal enforceability as between husband and wife. Furthermore they have been supported by the courts even where the promise of the man was to give property to a third person, other than the wife.[2] Also, the contractual liability has been held to survive the death of the promisor and to bind his estate.[3] In view of the universal recognition of the ante-nuptial agreement relating to property, both real estate and personalty, the question naturally arises as to the reason for the difficulty in recognizing and enforcing promises in the *Cautiones* relating to the baptism and education of children in mixed marriages. The answer is that agreements for the payment of money and agreements relating to the transfer or creation of a property interest in tangible property have not presented any difficulty in computation of the amount or in specific enforcement respectively.

In contrast, this ante-nuptial agreement presents a question distinct from tangible vested rights to money or property, or, as one judge has said in this regard, the right "is not a matter of property but a matter of feeling."[4] Because of this

[1] In using the term "right," I am not falling into the error of assuming what I attempt to prove. "Right" in this use is equivalent to "claim."

[2] Vason *v.* Bell, 53 Ga. 416 (1874).

[3] Dickinson *v.* Lane, 193 N. Y. 18; 85 N. E. 818 (1908).

[4] Andrews *v.* Salt, 8 Law Rep. Chancery App., 622, 628 note (1873).

fact, however, it is not less valuable to the parties concerned. On the contrary, the right is far more valuable and is connected in a very intimate way with the permanent contentment and happiness of the Catholic party to whom it is given. Our system of law has been historically divided into courts of law and courts of equity. Modern statutes have enlarged the sphere of jurisdiction of these courts giving both courts, but particularly the law courts, jurisdiction which formerly had been confined exclusively to the other. However, the principal distinction between the courts of law and courts of equity has been maintained, for the former limit their consideration to those matters in which the damages of the aggrieved party could be reduced to terms of money.[5] The latter—courts of equity—go beyond into the field of specific enforcement of contracts through the instrumentalities of negative injunctions which are issued against a person and forbid a certain line of conduct,[6] or of positive decrees which command the person affirmatively to act in a prescribed way.[7] Courts of equity have professed however to limit their consideration to cases which involve "property rights".[8] The truth of the profession has been challenged by learned authorities.[9] Even the casual reader will sense at once that some of the equity cases with which he is familiar, can at best be said to "hang on a peg" of technical property rights, for they actually deal substantially with personal rights, so-called rights of personality.

In the last half-century there has grown up a body of law which compels great respect and which has focussed the critical attention of legal scholars upon the out-worn theory that equity jurisdiction is limited to the adjudication of "property rights", substantial or technical in character. It has shown that the

[5] Pomeroy's Equity Jurisprudence (Students' Ed.), Sec. 139.

[6] *Ibidem*, Sec. 1337.

[7] *Ibidem*, Sec. 1359.

[8] See Chapter V.

[9] See Chapter V.

historical basis for the doctrine is questionable, and has attacked the court's use of fictions for the purpose of evading the real question of jurisdiction, often presented, that of the enforcement of a right of personality. This body of law marks a development which recommends itself for honesty and candor. It is a noteworthy step in the progress of the law. It recognizes a true situation in life—that rights exist, apart from property rights, which are extremely valuable and vital to the owner. It proceeds further to protect them upon the basic reasoning that the law *has inherent ability* to develop beyond the professed, technical, and unreasonable limitation established by precedent. It is submitted that the right, acquired by the Catholic party in the ante-nuptial agreement, to have the children baptized and reared in the Catholic religion is such a right of personality, and that it should be protected by the law even to the extent of specific enforcement by courts of equity. It is apparent to the reader that such ante-nuptial contracts cannot be effectively enforced in a court of law where the remedies are limited to money damages. It seems clear that damages in terms of money for the breach of such a contract are neither possible to compute nor adequate to compensate. The only other alternative is redress in a court of equity in the form of specific enforcement. It may be added here that, considered generally, the courts of equity have exclusive jurisdiction of matters concerning rights between husband and wife.[10] The function of equity in this regard is illustrated by the following:

> Courts of equity alone can give a remedy on a contract made between a husband and his wife, whether redress is sought by one of the original parties against the other or by or against the legal representative of one or both of the original parties.[11]

It is therefore submitted that since such promises are within the purview of modern extension of equity jurisdiction, and

[10] Woodruff *v.* Clark, 42 N. J. Law (13 Vr.) 198 (1880).

[11] See also Metzler *v.* Metzler, 8 N. J. Misc. R. 821; 151 A., 847 (1930).

since courts of law are unable to give adequate relief, equitable remedies should be granted upon analogy to modern cases which protect and secure interests of personality. Since this statement will probably be challenged, it is worth while to review briefly the theories of equity jurisdiction particularly in reference to protecting interests of personality. Some modern writers have classified the various individual interests and have set apart in a distinct division " rights of personality ", which they claim should be recognized and legally protected. For example, Dean Pound's classification is as follows:

> Individual interests may be classified as (a) interests of personality,—the individual physical and spiritual existence; (b) domestic interests,—expanded individual life, and (c) interests of substance, —the individual economic life.[12]

Further emphasis upon the recognition of interests of this character is shown by the same writer in the following:

> The (domestic) relations themselves are both personal and economic. Hence the individual interests therein partly involve the individual personality, the feelings, the affections, the honor of the individual, but also partly involve the individual substance so far as the relations incidentally give individual economic advantages. . . . (1) the first, as parents may urge it, should perhaps be put more broadly than Professor Wigmore needed to state it for the purposes of the law of torts. Parents may and do claim not merely the society of their children, as ministering a social pleasure, but the custody and control of them, especially while they are of tender years, and the power to dictate their training, prescribe their education and form their religious opinions. All those things are claimed, as it were, as a part of the parent's personality. (2) The chastity of a female child, also, is so intimately connected with the honor of the family and the self-respect and mental comfort of the parent, that the interest in maintaining it is asserted as a phase of the parent's interest of personality. . . . The first and second,

[12] R. Pound: Interests of Personality, 28 Harv. L. Rev., 343, 349 (1915).

as they are in the nature of interest of personality, encounter the difficulties involved in securing of personality through rules of law and judicial machinery. As to the first, the parent's interest in society and control of children is secured against strangers by the writ of habeas corpus, by the jurisdiction of courts of equity, preventive and remedial, and by an action for damages against one who interferes with the relation, in which the injury to the feelings of the parent, to a limited extent only, are made the basis of a reparation, as it were, parasitic to the claim for injury to the economic relation. But of late the law has put many limitations upon the parent's claim to custody of children and to control of their training and bringing up. . . . Finally these interests are in effect interests of personality, they are so peculiarly related to the mental and spiritual life of the individual as to involve in the highest degree the difficulties incident to all legal reparation of injuries to the person.[13]

Our legal system recognizes this unique relationship and predicates upon it very significant and unusual changes in legal rights. The Chief Justice of the Supreme Judicial Court of Massachusetts has said of one legal phase of this situation:

. . . At common law, without merit or fault in respect of his own conduct, the child was entitled to the benefit of his father's vigilance and forethought and was subject to all disadvantages resulting from any failure of performance of that parental duty. . . . This principle of law arises out of the family. It recognizes the parent in a sense as the repository of a trust to nurture and protect his offspring. It charges him with responsibility on that footing. The natural fact of entire dependence of so young a child upon the parent is thus adopted as the basis of legal rights and obligations. This principle is quite disconnected with the law of master and servant, host and guest, joint adventurers, or any other association of life. . . .[14]

And writing about the problem of redress where such rights

[13] R. Pound: Individual Interests in the Domestic Relations, 14 Mich. L. Rev., 177, 178, 183, 196 (1916).

[14] Gallagher *v.* Johnson, 237 Mass. 455, 130 N. E. 174 (1921).

have been violated, the learned writer describes the legal situation graphically in the following passages:

A man's feelings are as much a part of his personality as his limbs. The actions that protect the latter from injury may well be made to protect the former by the ordinary process of legal growth. The problems are rather to devise suitable redress and to limit the right in view of other interests involved. . . . In connection with interests of personality, where redress by way of damages is often obviously inadequate if not inapplicable, the hesitation of our law to apply preventive remedies is unfortunate and without just excuse. . . . It impairs the mental peace and comfort of the individual and may produce suffering much more acute than that produced by a mere bodily injury. . . .[15]

In striking agreement are these modern theories, propounded by such leaders of legal thought, with the earlier expressed teaching of Pope Leo XIII, when speaking of the relation of parent and child and the interests involved. He had declared many years before that the child is an "*extension of the person*" of the parents and that children "carry on, so to speak, and continue" that personality.[16]

While the Catholic religion places great emphasis upon the closeness of the relation between parent and child, it never views the result as a merger and appreciates and retains the individuality of each. It is commonplace to remark that a child resembles the parents in physical characteristics. But the one fact, which is sometimes overlooked, is the reality of the resemblance in mental and religious characteristics resulting from the influence of the parental relationship. This is recognized and emphasized in the religious belief of the Catholic.

But it may be objected that religious belief has not such a reality as could be appreciated and recognized by courts. How-

[15] R. Pound: Interests of Personality, 28 Harv. L. Rev., 343, 363, 364 (1915).

[16] Encyclical Letter *Rerum Novarum*, 15 May, 1891—*The Great Encyclical Letters of Leo XIII*, p. 246.

ever, this reality of religion as a real right of personality has been acknowledged in a striking way by a New York Court. In this case an orphaned child of Catholic parents, who was just 14 years old, was placed under the care of a Protestant by a married elder sister. The child's eldest brother, a Catholic, sought to be appointed guardian. It appears that the Protestant was financially able to care for the child and the brother was not so able. The child desired to remain with the Protestant. The court ordered the child to remain in the custody of the Protestant and that she be enducated in a Catholic residential institution.

In this case the justice writing the opinion said:

> *To Catholics, in particular, the education of an infant, leading as it does to their indissoluble marriage law, and their family relations founded on a subordination and respect to elders, the education (I say) of their infants in their own way is regarded by them as of paramount importance.*[17]

In another and very recent case from the same state Catholic parents in impecunious circumstances executed a contract relinquishing custody of two minor sons during minority to respondent, a Protestant, on condition that respondent would divide the earnings of the children as violinists and assume responsibility of the children's maintenance and musical education. Subsequently, the respondent was made a general guardian of the children and removed them to another state to advance their musical training. The father then sought to recover custody of the children. The court permitted the children to remain with the Protestant guardian but appointed a Catholic priest as co-guardian of the persons of the wards. The court, after quoting with approval of the language of the Mancini case above, said:

[17] Matter of Mancini, 89 Misc. Rep. 83, 86; 151 N. Y. Supp., 387, 389 (1915). (Italics inserted.)

. . . it is important that the spiritual education of children of such an impressionable age should be properly safeguarded. It is conceded that the wishes of their parents to have them brought up in the religion of their ancestors must be respected. And this is also the view which the law takes. It does so, not as a matter of sentiment or out of deference to narrow sectarian views, but as a matter of sound public policy. The family is the institutional unit in which infants, the cooperation between the home, the school, and the church or other spiritual agency, can best be prepared as members of society and as good citizens. Even though the infant be physically separate from the family, it is still constructively a part of it, and entitled to be brought up in the religious faith professed by its parents. These principles are entirely consistent with the American view of religious liberty.[18]

The courts in these decisions have recognized the fact that religion is a reality in the life of the individual and thus agreed with the conclusions of all great psychologists.

William James refers to the problem in the following brilliant language:

All our attitudes, moral, practical, or emotional, as well as religious, are due to the "objects" of our consciousness, the things which we believe to exist, whether really or ideally, along with ourselves. Such objects may be present to our senses, or they may be present only to our thought. In either case they elicit from us a reaction; and the reaction due to things of thought is notoriously in many cases as strong as that due to sensible presences.[19]

Another passage reads:

For when all is said and done, we are in the end absolutely dependent on the universe; and into sacrifices and surrenders of some sort, deliberately looked at and accepted, we are drawn and pressed as into our only permanent positions of repose. Now in those

[18] People *v.* Lackey, 248 N. Y. Supp., 561 (1930).

[19] William James, *The Varieties of Religious Experience* (New York: Longmans, Green, and Co., 1925), p. 53.

states of mind which fall short of religion, the surrender is submitted to as an imposition of necessity, and the sacrifice is undergone at the very best without complaint. In the religious life, on the contrary, surrender and sacrifice are positively espoused: even unnecessary givings-up are added in order that the happiness may increase. *Religion thus makes easy and felicitous what in any case is necessary;* and if it be the only agency that can accomplish this result, its vital importance as a human faculty stands vindicated beyond dispute. It becomes an essential organ of our life, performing a function which no other portion of our nature can so successfully fulfill. From the merely biological point of view, so to call it, this conclusion to which, so far as I can now see, we shall inevitably be led, and led moreover by following the purely empirical method of demonstration which I sketched to you in the first lecture.[20]

An eminent English psychologist discusses the conception in this fashion:

And therefore at bottom popular feeling is right in holding that religious belief is necessary to Morality. Of course I do not mean to say that, were religious belief to disappear from the world, morality would disappear too. But I do think Morality would become quite a different thing from what it has been for the higher levels of religious thought and feeling. The best men would no doubt go on acting up to their own highest ideal just as if it did not possess objective validity, no matter how unable they might be to reconcile their practical with their speculative beliefs. But it would not be so for the many, or perhaps even for the few in their moments of weakness and temptation, when once the consequences of purely naturalistic Ethics were thoroughly admitted and realized.[21]

The universal acceptance of the reality of religion is pointed out by another leading philosopher:

There is hardly an aspect of our changing life with which religion

[20] William James, *op. cit.*, pp. 51, 52.

[21] Hastings Rashdall, *Philosophy and Religion* (New York: Charles Scribner's Sons, 1910), p. 75.

does not come into touch and which it may not bless and consecrate. . . . Confirmation, Holy Communion, Marriage or Holy Orders, Extreme Unction, and Burial in the Catholic practice, . . . these are but practical applications and noble symbols of the fact, that religion is almost as many-sided and inclusive as life.[22]

And how embracing is the effect upon the individual's relationship with all phases of his life, finds expression in another excellent work:

The religious feelings of mature life center most naturally about three things: the sense of one's own spiritual life, the consciousness of the larger life outside the self, and an appreciation of the relationship existing between the self and this larger life.[23]

Finally, modern philosophical thought has found expression in this short passage from Pratt:

In short, religion is not a theory about reality; it *is* a reality. And yet we must not forget that it is a reality which includes a theory.[24]

These opinions have been taken from outside the Catholic Church. The Church's position on the point is very clearly exemplified in the words of St. Thomas Aquinas:

Again, we must observe that, in the human species, the offspring needs not only nourishment for its body, as with other animals, but also instruction for its soul. For other animals have their natural forethought which enables them to provide for themselves: whereas man lives by reason, which can attain to forethought only after long experience: so that children need to be instructed by their parents who are experienced.

Moreover children are not capable of this instruction as soon as they are born, but only after a long time, and especially when they

[22] James Bissett Pratt, *The Religious Consciousness* (New York: The Macmillan Company, 1920), p. 121.

[23] Edwin Diller Starbuck, *The Psychology of Religion* (London: Walter Scott, 1899), p. 324.

[24] James Bissett Pratt, *The Religious Consciousness*, p. 7.

reach the age of discretion. Besides, this instruction requires a long time. And even then, on account of the assaults of the passions whereby the judgment of prudence is perverted, they need not only instruction but correction.[25]

It is submitted without hesitation that the additional right acquired by the Catholic to have the children baptized and brought up as Catholics is so intimately connected with the parent's existence, religious conviction, and individual contentment and satisfaction, that it may be properly described as an interest in personality. Now, the ante-nuptial agreement has been made with the non-Catholic party fully aware of the religious belief of the Catholic. Free to accept or reject the agreement he or she has chosen to accept and, upon the strength of the promises contained in it, the Catholic has changed his or her status irrevocably. Married life has a supernatural purpose to the Catholic parent. The begetting of children, their baptism and religious training have a meaning of tremendous spiritual import to the Catholic party. This is not said in disparagement of the non-Catholic. It is said to emphasize the fact that religious truths are of the very fibre of life's existence to the Catholic. And, since the very *raison d'être* of the ante-nuptial agreement is the religious conviction and status of the Catholic party, it is essential to pause and review his religious beliefs as they form a part of the ante-nuptial agreement. From childhood he (or she) has been taught that every human being is a creature of God, with a definite purpose in life and a part of the divine plan. Neither the so-called liberty of adult age, prosperity, power, or intellectual achievement, enlarge, narrow or change the purpose of life which he has learned in the beginners' Catechism; viz., "God made me to know Him, to love Him, and to serve Him in this world, and to be happy with Him forever in Heaven." God grants spiritual regeneration in Bap-

[25] St. Thomas Aquinas, *The Summa Contra Gentiles*, 3rd Book, Part II, Chap. 122, pp. 112, 113. (Burnes, Oates & Washbourne).

tism, and all through life communicates His spiritual powers to the individual soul through the sacraments. The individual's rôle is accurately described by an authoritative Catholic writer in the following passage:

> Our role consists in making use of the divine gifts in order to live with God and for God, in order to live in union with Jesus and to imitate Him. But we cannot live that supernatural life without a continual struggle against the threefold concupiscence which still remains in us. And moreover, since God has endowed us with a supernatural organism, it is our duty to make that life increase in us by meritorious acts and the fervent reception of the sacraments.[26]

The meaning of the sacraments as a living vital force is explained as follows:

> We have already shown how the seven sacraments of the Church embrace the whole of human life, and how they sanctify all its heights and depths. The soul at peace with God is sanctified in Confirmation and Holy Eucharist; the soul burdened with sin in Baptism and Penance; the afflicted soul, in the awful hour of death, in the Last Anointing. The community life also is sanctified by the sacramental blessing; on its social side by the sacrament of Matrimony, on its religious side by the sacrament of Holy Orders. It is before all else the realism of its sacramental thought which gives the sacramental worship of the Church its religious and moral value. The Church does not attenuate the sacrament into an empty symbol, or into a sign of grace which obtains all its efficacy from subjective faith. On the contrary it is a real expression of Our Lord's gracious will, a sign of Christ (signum Christi), and as such it already ensures the presence of His grace through itself, through its actual performance. That is a fundamental point of Catholic sacramental doctrine. "A sacrament is not fulfilled by the fact that one believes in it, but by the fact that it is performed." (Sacramenta non implentur dum creduntur, sed dum fiunt.) Thus through the sacraments the divine wins tangible reality and becomes a visible and

[26] Adolphe Tanquerey, S.S., *The Spiritual Life* (Tournai: Desclée and Co., 1930), p. 45.

present value. Therefore the Catholic has an immediate experience of the divine, an experience as immediate and objective as is the child's experience of the love of its mother.[27]

And likewise the Catholic party has been taught the steadfast truth that marriage is a holy sacrament, instituted by Christ, in which a man and woman are united forever to achieve in primary end the procreation and education of children and as secondary end their mutual support.[28] And the meaning of marriage and life itself is explained in an address to the couple to be married, frequently used at the very ceremony in which these parties become man and wife.[29]

[27] Karl Adam, *The Spirit of Catholicism* (New York: The Macmillan Co., 1931), p. 185; Tilmann Pesch, *The Christian Philosophy of Life* (London: Sands and Co., 1909), p. 369; "Rights and Duties of Parents", *The Catholic Mind*, Vol. 23 (1925), p. 321; "The Catholic Home", *op. cit.*, Vol. 27 (1929), pp. 290, 294; Spirago-Clarke, *The Catechism Explained* (New York: Benziger Brothers, 1927), p. 659; W. Wilmers, S.J., *Handbook of the Christian Religion* (3rd ed., New York: Benziger Brothers), p. 483.

[28] H. A. Ayrinhac, *Marriage Legislation in the New Code of Canon Law* (Revised ed., J. P. Lydon—New York: Benziger Brothers, 1932), p. 23. J. D. Malloy, C.S.P., *A Catechism for Inquirers* (4th ed., New York: The Paulist Press, 1927), p. 51, teaches:

"(10) MATRIMONY

"144. By whom was Matrimony instituted?

"Matrimony was instituted by God Himself, ..."

[29] "My dear friends: You are about to enter into a union which is most sacred and most serious. It is most sacred, because established by God Himself; most serious, because it will bind you together for life in a relationship so close and so intimate that it will profoundly influence your whole future. That future with its hopes and disappointments, its successses and its failures, its pleasures and its pains, its joys and its sorrows, is hidden from your eyes. You know that these elements are mingled in every life, and are to be expected in your own.

"And so not knowing what is before you, you take each other for better or for worse, for richer or for poorer, in sickness and in health, until death. ... Truly, then, these words are most serious. It is a beautiful tribute to your undoubted faith in each other, that recognizing their full import, you are nevertheless so willing and ready to pronounce them. And because these words involve such solemn obligations, it is most fitting that you rest the

The duty of Family Life, in Catholic doctrine, is more than a mere human convenience. Its dignity and meaning are explained by a noted Catholic theologian as follows:

The family is a Divine institution, and God has willed that the majority of men shall be subject to the obligations which it necessarily implies. . . .

Happiness is only to be found in a home where God is Master, and all are concerned to do His will. In this regard Christ is our perfect example. . . .

The whole structure of human society has its foundations in the home, and man's weal or woe depends upon the manner of the child's upbringing there. It is the father, even more than the mother, who must be held answerable for the faithful discharge of this task.

The conduct of parents, and more particularly the example set by the mother in the home, must necessarily be a potent formative influence in a child's life.[80]

security of your wedded life upon the great principle of self-sacrifice. And so you begin your married life by the voluntary and complete surrender of your individual lives in the interest of that deeper and wider life which you are to have in common.

"Henceforth you will belong entirely to each other; you will be one in mind, one in heart, and one in affections. And whatever sacrifices you may hereafter be required to make to preserve this common life, always make them generously. Sacrifice is usually difficult and irksome. Only love can make it easy; and perfect love can make it a joy. We are willing to give in proportion as we love. And when love is perfect the sacrifice is complete. . . .

"No greater blessing can come to your married life than pure conjugal love, loyal and true to the end. May, then, this love with which you join your hands and hearts today never fail, but grow deeper and stronger as the years go on. And if true love and the unselfish spirit of perfect sacrifice guide your every action, you can expect the greatest measure of earthly happiness that may be allotted to man in this vale of tears. The rest is in the hands of God. Nor will God be wanting to your needs; He will pledge you the life-long support of His graces in the Holy Sacrament which you are now going to receive."—*The Ritual for the Celebration of Matrimony, Instruction Before Marriage.*

[80] Tilmann Pesch, S.J., *The Christian Philosophy of Life*, pp. 369-370.

Parenthood and the religious training of children have been made equally clear.[31]

A casual examination of these representative writers concerning Catholic doctrine will suffice to impress upon the reader the added reasons which may fairly be stressed to support the contention, that the right acquired by the Catholic in the ante-nuptial agreement is not only a right but the most obvious kind of right of personality.

[31] "Religious knowledge is the most important for the pupil, because, above all, we are creatures of God, and are therefore bound to worship and obey Him as our Creator. Our duties to God stand before all our other duties, and the knowledge and worship of God must ever be first among the obligations arising in the dawning intelligence of the child. But it is impossible for the child to acquire a due knowledge of God and of his obligations towards Him in a few lessons, or within a few weeks or months. Time is needed, as with all other branches of knowledge. Progress can be made only step by step. Hence, the work of teaching religion should occupy the place of first importance in the education of the child and should be, as far as possible, continuous...."—J. A. Burns, C.S.C., *Catholic Education* (New York: Longmans, Green and Co., 1917), p. 22.

"Parents are under very grave obligation, according to their means, to attend to the education of their children, both religious and moral, physical and civil, and also to provide for their temporal good."

"This obligation is imposed upon parents by the very law of nature; canon law reaffirms, defines, and enforces it. The Catholic Church has always maintained that the rights and duties of parents extend to all the functions of education. As far as depends on them, they are bound to make their children strong and good men and women, good Christians and good citizens. They should look after their temporal welfare, principally when children are not able to provide for themselves, but afterward, also, to help them to improve their social condition."—H. A. Ayrinhac, *Marriage Legislation in the New Code of Canon Law*, p. 277.

CHAPTER V

The Remedy of Specific Enforcement of the Right of Personality

If, as has just been pointed out, the ante-nuptial agreement fulfills the legal requirements of a contract and results in an added right of personality to the Catholic party, the further question remains whether such an interest of personality should be given the protection of specific performance in equity in view of existing authorities. Such a sanction, it may be objected, needs the support of convincing legal authorities. It was pointed out earlier that some equity courts still cling to the old traditional principle that courts of equity recognize only "property rights," substantial or technical, as the limited basis of their jurisdiction. But that narrow basis of equitable relief has been subjected to sharp attack for many years. The growing trend of judicial decisions and legal scholarship shows an increasing departure from the traditional basis and a tendency to extend the protection given to rights of personality. All discussions of this question run back to the dictum of Lord Eldon in the famous case of Gee *v.* Pritchard decided in 1818.[1] In that case the plaintiff's late husband had educated and brought up the defendant in the family as an adopted son. After the death of the husband, the defendant, dissatisfied with the provisions of the will, threatened to publish letters which had been written to him as a member of the family by the plaintiff. Lord Eldon continued the injunction against the publication. But he said that the remedy was granted on the ground that the plaintiff had a " sufficient property in the

[1] R. Pound: Equitable Relief against Defamation and Injuries to Personality, 29 Harv. L. Rev., 640 (1916).

original letters to authorize an injunction," and added the much-quoted dictum. That dictum is generally regarded among legal students as the basis of the traditional principle. It states that relief in equity can rest only upon property rights and not upon any injury to feelings or other interests in personality. The soundness of the influence of this dictum in subsequent cases has been questioned by a great authority in these words:

> Do the rules which our books still announce upon this subject rest upon any basis more legitimate than unintelligent adherence to the dicta of a great judge in the pioneer case?
>
> It will have been perceived that the real injury in Gee *v.* Pritchard was an invasion of the right of privacy. In result therefore, a case in which we are told that equity has no jurisdiction to secure interests of personality, and the case always cited since for that proposition, was a pioneer decision finding a way for securing the then unknown right of privacy.[2]

The more enlightened courts have definitely broken away from the influence of Lord Eldon's dictum and recognized in an emphatic way the sound basis for equitable relief which exists in cases involving personality rights. This trend has been noted in a scholarly article:

> This development of the law was inevitable. The intense intellectual and emotional life, and the heightening of sensations which came with the advance of civilization, made it clear to men that only a part of the pain, pleasure, and profits of life lay in physical things. Thoughts, emotions, and sensations demanded legal recognition, and the beautiful capacity for growth which characterizes the common law enabled the judges to afford the requisite protection, without the interposition of the legislature.[3]

An eminent teacher in equity has further described the evolution of the trend:

[2] R. Pound, *op. cit.*, 29 Harv. L. Rev., 641, 642 (1915).

[3] Samuel D. Warren and Louis D. Brandeis: The Right to Privacy, 4 Harv. L. Rev., 193, 195 (1890).

Dean Pound renewed the attack on a still broader front. Each year brings increasing evidence that their views will eventually be accepted by courts and legislatures. The law courts from early times have protected interests of personality, for example, by actions of slander and libel. What rational principle forbids the application to such rights of the familiar rule that if there is a remedy at law which is inadequate, then equity gives relief, unless special considerations restrain the exercise of its jurisdiction.[4]

An examination of a few of the leading cases will show the development of this commendable doctrine, that equity is not restricted by any artificial limitation as to jurisdiction based upon substantial or technical property rights. On the contrary it has ample inherent jurisdiction to proceed to the protection of rights of personality through the issuance of affirmative orders and negative injunctions.

This may be illustrated by a review of a few of the leading cases. In *Ex Parte Warfield* the plaintiff brought an action in equity against the defendant, alleging that the defendant was causing a partial alienation of affections of plaintiff's wife. The petitioner asked that the defendant be restrained from visiting or associating with her, writing or speaking to her or in any manner communicating with her. The defendant was subsequently committed to jail for contempt of court in violating the terms of the court's order. He attacked the validity of the injunction by suing out a writ of habeas corpus to test the legality of his imprisonment. In such a proceeding the question of the jurisdiction of the equity court is always of prime importance. The court denied relief and remanded the defendant to custody.

The case turns upon the husband's right to the undisturbed enjoyment of the consortium of his spouse. Another court, speaking of this right, has said:

[4] Z. Chafee, Jr.: The Progress of the Law—The Extension of Equitable Jurisdiction Beyond the Protection of Property Rights, 34 Harv. L. Rev., 388, 407 (1921).

The right of either husband or wife to the consortium of their respective spouse, as distinguished from the right of service belonging to the husband or the right to support belonging to the wife, has been regarded as of a somewhat sentimental character. Yet this right of consortium has been treated by a number of courts as a species of property.[5]

It may be objected that the jurisdiction of equity in *Ex Parte Warfield* was enlarged by statute or that consortium is a property right; but to do this is to reach out for the basis of a technical "property right however slender and shadowy." It is clear that the real basis was the right of the husband to an undisturbed possession of his right of personality acquired by marriage.[6] As the court of appeal said:

It cannot be seriously questioned that the principal object of the suit was to preserve the marital relations existing between plaintiff and his spouse, and to conserve as as far as may be, and rehabiliate her affections for the plaintiff.[7]

A Supreme Court, whose decisions are often cited with approval, has in a case protecting a right of personality indi-

[5] Larisa *v.* Tiffaffny, 42 R. I., 148; 105 A, 739, 743 (1919).

[6] *Ex parte* Warfield, 40 Tex. Crim. Appeals 413; 50 S. W. 933 (1899).

[7] A contrary opinion was announced in a New York case. In this case the husband secured a divorce in Mexico which was held void by a New York court. He then married another woman in Connecticut and returned to New York. The lower court enjoined, on the petition of the first wife, the second wife from holding herself out as married to the husband. It also restrained the husband from holding out that he had secured a divorce, and further restrained the woman from using the name of the husband and forbade them to go through any marriage ceremony while the plaintiff wife was living. The Superior Court, in reversing the lower court's decision, said:

"Equity cannot by injunction restrain conduct which merely injures a person's feelings and causes mental anguish.... The law does not remedy all social evils or moral wrongs. In the case of Atkinson *v.* Doherty, 121 Mich. 372, the court said: 'Although injuries to feelings are recognized as a ground for increasing damages, the law has never given a right of action for an injury to feelings merely.'"—Baumann *v.* Baumann, 250 N. Y. Rep. 382; 165 N. E. 819 (1929). (Cardozo, C.J., did not vote.)

cated its agreement with this view. Here we had a petition by a husband against his wife, who was separated from him, and against the wife's child, alleging that his wife fraudulently claimed that the child was his son and had caused such fact to be noted on the city's vital statistics record. The bill prayed for a permanent injunction against the wife and infant, restraining them from claiming for the child under their certificate the "status, name, property or privilege" of a lawful child. While in that case the court found a property interest remotely involved, and made it the "technical basis" of equity jurisdiction, yet the court proceeded to state clearly that, even in the absence of property rights, it would hold rights of personality as a sufficient basis for equity jurisdiction. The opinion contains the following language:

> If it appeared in this case that only the complainant's status and personal rights were thus threatened or thus invaded by the action of the defendants and by the filing of the false certificate, we should hold, and without hesitation, that an individual has rights, other than property rights, which he can enforce in a court of equity and which a court of equity will enforce against invasion, and we should declare that the complainant was entitled to relief.[8]

This plain statement by the court is commendable. It has been approved in these words:

> Moreover the remarks of the court on the subject of equitable protection of interests of personality are admirable and will undoubtedly exert a wholesome influence.[9]

While equity's jurisdiction over dead bodies may be said to rest upon a quasi property right, wishes of the deceased and particularly the religious feelings have been respected by the

[8] Dill, J., in Vanderbilt *v.* Mitchell, 72 N. J. Eq. 910; 67 Atl. 97, 100 (1907).

[9] Comment on above opinion by R. Pound, *op. cit.*, 29 Harv. L. Rev., 640, 677 (1916).

courts. Now the following language of a leading American jurist, Mr. Justice Cardozo as Chief Judge of the New York Court, forbidding the removal of the body of a Catholic from consecrated ground, gives an idea of the proper approach to evaluating the strong convictions and deep sentiment of the Catholic's religious belief:

> In the faith of the Church, plaintiff's mother and brother were buried in the plot so purchased. This was done some years ago while Mr. Yome was yet alive. . . . On his deathbed he received the sacraments of the Church, and he was laid in his grave in accordance with its rites. A rule of the Church forbids the removal of a body from consecrated ground to ground that is unconsecrated, or consecrated to another faith. . . .
>
> Defendants remind us on the other hand that he was reared in the faith of the Church, and died in it, sending for a priest upon his deathbed to gain the privilege of burial in consecrated ground.
>
> Even without contract, sentiments and usages, devoutly held as sacred, may not be flouted for caprice. They must be weighed in the balance with the motives and feelings that sway the acts of the survivors.[10]

The case of Stark *v.* Hamilton follows the trend of authority favoring rights of personality as a sufficient basis for equity jurisdiction. In this case the defendant seduced the plaintiff's minor daughter. The plaintiff sought to enjoin the defendant from associating with the girl. The court granted the injunction, saying:

> The principal case might also have been decided as involving a property right. The plaintiff could have maintained an action at law for the loss of his daughter's services. . . . But the court does not rest its jurisdiction on this property interest, but upon the interests of personality which are really at stake.[11]

[10] Cardozo, J., in Yome *v.* Gorman, 242 N. Y. 395; 152 N. E. 126, 128, 129 (1926).

[11] Stark *v.* Hamilton, 149 Ga. 44; 99 S. E. 40 (1918).

The candor and reasoning of this court has been rightly praised.

This decision might have found an incidental property right in the father's interest in his daughter's services, but refuses to hang such a property " peg ".[12]

And Professor Chafee approves this passage from the opinion:

It is difficult to understand why injunctive protection of a mere property right should be placed above similar protection from the continual humiliation of the father and the reputation of the family. In some instances the former may be adequately compensated in damages, but the latter is irreparable; for no mere money consideration could restore the good name and reputation of the family, or palliate the humiliation of the father for the continual debauching of his daughter.[13]

This same principle is rightly developed by Justice Cardozo *in his Growth of the Law:*

I find again in a recent judgment of my own court the case that points my meaning. We held a little while ago in Oppenheim *v.* Kridel, 236 N. Y. 156, that a woman, as well as a man, may maintain an action for criminal conversation. The court of intermediate appeal had ruled that the action would not lie. To make out the woman's disability, precedents were cited from the time of Lord Coke. Stress was laid upon pronouncements in those days that a man had a property right in the body of his wife. A wife, it was said, had none in the body of her husband. Stress was laid also upon ruling made in days when the wife was unable, unless the husband joined with her as plaintiff, to sue for any wrong. We did not ignore these precedents, but we held them inconclusive. Social, political, and legal reforms had changed the relations between the sexes, and put woman and man upon a plane of equality. Decisions founded upon the assumption of a bygone inequality were unrelated to present-day realities, and ought not to be permitted

[12] Chafee: The Progress of the Law, Equitable Relief against Torts, 34 Harv. L. Rev., 388, 413 (1921).

[13] *Ibidem.*

to prescribe a rule of life. (*Cf.* R. *v.* Jackson, 1891, I. Q. B. 671.) The historical method was the organon of judgment in each court.[14]

Any further hesitancy to protect such rights by equity courts is not easy to comprehend; for the law has reached a point where recognition of the fictions formerly employed is gradually enlarging and the analogy as to the value of the services of a minor daughter disappearing. It is more apparent that, if the father were extremely wealthy and the child poor, the father would still be able to protect the personality right which he enjoys toward the child. The same is true if the child is wealthy and the parent poor. The real reason is that there is no actual property right in the old sense present in a suit of this character.

Legal scholars see in these cases that:

> There is distinctly discernible a tendency on the part of the courts to afford a more adequate protection to personal rights.[15]

The persistence of some courts in masking the protection of such rights by seeking an appearance of substantial or shadowy property rights as the basis of jurisdiction is not helpful in the progress of the law and is illustrative of a method which should be deprecated vigorously.[16]

In giving affirmative relief, courts of equity show a sound tendency to supply needed protection. This need is well expressed in an introduction to a recent case-book on the subject:

> The growing complexity of human relations and the increasing power of government officials over the activities of citizens afford abundant opportunity for wrongs which disturb the liberty and

[14] Cardozo, *The Growth of the Law*, Chap. IV, pp. 105-106 (1924).

[15] T. D. Theobald: Does Equity Protect Property Rights in Domestic Relations, 19 Ken. L. Journ., 1, 57, 59 (1930).

[16] J. Frank, *Law and the Modern Mind*, Chap. VI, p. 237 (1930). "Hesitant avowal has begotten conduct that is spasmodic and irregular; there has been a feeling, inarticulate to some extent, that the conduct was something to be deprecated, something calling for excuse."

emotional life of the individual as well as his control over property. Situations constantly arise which are too delicate to be satisfactorily handled in actions for damages. They call for the flexibility of prevention and other specific relief, if only practical obstacles and the barriers of precedent are overcome.[17]

In summarizing the present state of the authorities, we may adopt the language of a leading American digest:

The variety of cases above referred to in which personal rights are really protected by courts of equity shows that, while it is a commonly accepted theory that their jurisdiction must rest upon rights of property, there are at least many exceptions to the rule. Among them cases of contract, trust, or breach of confidence relating to personal rights, cases respecting the education and custody of children, and cases relating to the right of privacy and reputation, such as those restraining the publication or exhibition of photographs or other representations of the person and the publication of private letters. In addition to these are the cases relating to the security of the person and the protection of health and physical comfort. While in many of these cases the jurisdiction is nominally based on an alleged property right, it is plain that the observance of the rule that equity will be limited to rights of property is little more than nominal. In all this class of cases equity does concern itself about personal rights as the real subject of consideration.[18]

[17] Preface to "Cases on Equitable Relief against Defamation and Injuries to Personality," by Roscoe Pound. Introd. by Z. Chafee, Jr., p. 3 (1930).

[18] 37 L. R. A. 787 (1897). *Cf.* also J. R. Long, in 33 Yale Law Journal, 115, 116, 117, 132 (1923), who says:

"The jurisdiction of equity does not properly depend upon the nature of the right involved, whether a right of person or of property; the sure test of equity jurisdiction is the existence of a justifiable right for which there is not a full, adequate, and complete remedy at law.

"At any rate cases involving personal rights are becoming common in courts of equity, and the doctrine that these courts have no jurisdiction to protect such rights is being discarded before it had become really established by judicial action....

"From this review it must be clear that the doctrine that a court of equity has no jurisdiction to protect personal rights is unsound in principle and

This has been approved in a leading case [19] on the subject and has likewise been approved by a foremost scholar: [20]

It is submitted in conclusion that the promises of the ante-nuptial agreement, fulfilling as they do all the formal requirements of a civil contract, and giving an added right of personality to the Catholic party, should be and will be enforced by courts of equity, which are drawing away from historical, artificial limitations of jurisdiction and progressing with a sound legal appreciation of the inherent capacity of the law to develop with the needs of the present.

unsupported by controlling authority. Originating in what appears to be a mistake as to the real significance of the existence of a property right as a jurisdictional fact,—namely, that it justifies the court in taking cognizance of cases otherwise beyond its jurisdiction, it has not as yet had the support of a single case known to the writer in which the denial of equitable relief was based squarely and solely on the ground that the right involved was a personal right. On the other hand, there has already accumulated a respectable body of decisions in which courts of equity have protected personal rights, either frankly dealt with as such or thinly camouflaged as property rights. It would seem that the time has come for the courts to discard this unsound dogma, which while it has probably never caused a denial of justice in actual decisions, stands in the way of the logical and symmetrical development of the law by courts of equity."

[19] *Ex parte* Warfield, 40 Tex. Crim. Appeals, 413; 50 S. W. 933 (1899).

[20] R. Pound: See various writings, *supra.*

CHAPTER VI

The Situation When One or Both Parents are Deceased

Practically all the cases, both English and American, as has been pointed out in a prior chapter, have arisen after one or both parents were dead. This fact has caused in a large measure the resulting confusion of precedent. It has complicated the original question relating to the enforceability of the agreement, with further troublesome problems of custody. The question of the enforceability of the agreement may arise independently of custody, as, for example, when both parents are living. It may also arise in intimate connection with the problem of determining to whom custody shall be given, as, for example, when one or both parents are deceased. The law has become well settled that " best welfare of the child " is the determining factor in the award of custody of a child. Both English and American courts have adopted this principle.[1] And numerous court decisions and authoritative writers state that all other considerations yield to this criterion.[2] But " welfare of the child " is a very general term. The elements of religious training, physical comfort and support, education, environment, and many other forces produce the vague composite of " best welfare." The relative importance of these different elements has not been definitely appraised or defined by the courts, and courts have variously evaluated the element

[1] Schouler, *Domestic Relations* (5th ed.), Sec. 305 & Sec. 332. Peck, *Domestic Relations* (3rd ed.), Part 4, Guardian and Ward, Chap. 19, Sec. 150, p. 419.

[2] 41 L. R. A. (New Series), 564, 570; 31 Corpus Juris, 990 seq. Tiffany, *Domestic Relations* (2nd ed.), Sec. 125, p. 267; Sec. 156, p. 324. Maddan, *Persons and Domestic Relations*, Part 3, Guardian and Ward, Chap. 11, Sec. 153, p. 466.

of the religious training. They have not hesitated to say that the religious element is not the determining factor:

> The first and paramount duty is to consult the welfare of the child. The wishes of the parent as to the religious education . . . are entitled to weight; if nothing is put into the balance against them, ordinarily they will be decisive. If, however, those wishes cannot be carried into effect without sacrificing what the courts sees to be for the welfare of the child, they must so far be disregarded. The Court will not itself prefer one Church to another, but will act without bias for the welfare of the child under the circumstances of each case.[3]

And the same court speaking some years later said:

> Doubtless in cases of controverted custody due weight should be given to parental relations and desires, but the controlling consideration is the present and future interests of the child . . . and, although the wishes of the petitioner, who is the surviving parent, as to the religious training and environment of his daughter, should not be desregarded, we are unable to say . . . that the respondent should be removed where it seems . . . that the ward's welfare and happiness do not at present require the change. . . .[4]

The lack of any uniform standard by which courts might measure the weight to be given to the element of religious membership and religious training in proceedings determining custody has led courts into the utmost confusion. In some cases they have avoided such an appraisal altogether. In others they have failed properly to estimate it, or have acted without hesitation against the wishes and rights of the parents. Moreover, this confusion lies not only in decisions of different states but as well in decisions of courts in the same state. The following court opinions illustrate this confusion.

The New York Court has said:

[3] Purinton *v.* Jamrock, 195 Mass. 187; 80 N. E. 802, 805 (1907).

[4] Harding *v.* Brown, 227 Mass. 77; 117 N. E. 638, 640 (1917).

. . . the courts will, . . . take into consideration, . . . religious bringing up and teaching. . . . But . . . the consideration of temporal advantages in such cases controls over the religious.[5]

Another court of the same state, supporting the legal right of the father to have his child brought up in the same religion changed custody to effect that result.[6] In this case the father had been guilty of desertion and minor criminal offenses and was deemed generally untrustworthy. The mother was insane and the child had been committed to the care and education of a Protestant family. Guardianship was changed to the Catholic grandmother. In referring to the phase of the question arising out of the religion of the mother, the Court said:

During the period of immaturity incident to infancy the father and mother are the natural guardians of their children. They must shield them from dangers and temptations that beset not only their physical and moral but also their spiritual welfare. It is for them to lead in the path of a religion of their own choosing. If they agree, no question can arise; but here a case of disagreement is claimed. Both parties were Catholics. They were married in the Catholic faith. The ancestry of the children, so far as is known, is Roman Catholic. . . . All authorities agree that the expressed wish of the parents of a child, and particularly of the father, should have great weight with the court in the appointment of a guardian. The question of religion seems to have been involved in that case. While the ancient doctrine of patria potestas is only now an historical fact, and the common-law merger of the existence of the wife into that of her husband has ceased, while the wife is now in most respects the legal equal of her husband, yet the headship of the husband in the family is something more than mere sentiment. It is his name which is perpetuated, and his character should shape the conduct, and his ability achieve the success of the household. In the nature of things, it must still remain true that the father,

[5] People *v.* Woolston, 239 N. Y. Supp. 185, 188 (1929).

[6] *In re* Jacquet, 82 N. Y. Supp. 986 (1903).

though not in a tyrannical or opprobious way, should be the head of the family. . . .[7]

This does not change or weaken the statements made earlier concerning the enforceability of the agreement. For in this case no agreement existed.

In another case in the same state, the court had again to determine the question in proceeding to determine custody. A Catholic man had married a Baptist. She had died. In considering the award of custody the court found the father unworthy, but in giving custody to a Catholic woman and Protestant aunt prescribed that the child should be brought up in the Catholic religion. In its opinion, referred to before, the court speaking of English precedents said:

> This is a land where all forms of religion are both free and protected, and where the rights of fathers, within the law, are still recognized and applicable in proper cases. . . . These are tremendous differences, and thus it is that the common law of the people of this state and that of modern England are often very far apart in principle and in application. As the Romans looked upon themselves, and not modern Greece, as the true succession of ancient Greek thought, so our courts are obliged to assume that they and not the English courts, are the true interpreters of the great principles of the statute law once common to all English-speaking peoples, some few dependencies excepted. This assumption is a necessary corollary of sovereignty.[8]

These decisions, and particularly those taken from one state differing widely as they do, are typical. They show an utter lack of uniformity in the appraisal of religious training as an element in determining custody. In such confusion the estimate becomes largely governed by the belief and the personality of the particular judge. "Best welfare," then, has become a flexible term, changing with the point of view of the time,

[7] *In re* Jacquet, 82 N. Y. Supp. 986, 987, 988 (1903).

[8] *In re* Lamb's Estate, 139 N. Y. Supp. 685, 687, 690 (1912).

place and composition of the court. It is an elastic conception which confers an extremely broad discretion upon the judge and gives him the opportunity to superimpose his norm of general welfare and the relative importance of religion for that of the parents. This is illustrated by two proceedings in which the ante-nuptial agreement had been executed. In a Kansas case, Denton *v.* James,[9] a Protestant had signed the agreement before marrying a Catholic woman. She died after the birth of a child. An agreement was executed giving joint custody to the Catholic maternal grandparent and Protestant paternal grandparent. Without notice to the Catholic grandparent, the father and Protestant paternal grandparent secured the legal adoption of the child by the Protestant grandparent. The Catholic grandmother contested the validity of the adoption. The court sustained the adoption. The decision is curious because the court called attention to the fact that father and mother had equal authority and right in controlling the upbringing of the child, yet proceeded to close its eyes to the fact that the father had yielded his right by agreement. The court seems also to have overlooked the fact that the woman had changed her status, relying upon that agreement. Burch, J., in delivering the court's opinion, treats the agreement in these words:

> The agreement of the child's father and mother that the child should be reared in the Catholic faith was a commendable compromise between two natural guardians who, under the statute of this state, had equal authority. On the death of the mother, the father's right to educate his child became paramount, and the agreement was merely persuasive upon him.[10]

" Persuasive " in this meaning is a colorless term, possessed of no more than the popular meaning and sterile of legal force. Some states have attempted to curb judges in over-riding the

[9] Denton *v.* James, 107 Kansas 729; 193 Pac. 307 (1920).

[10] Denton *v.* James, *supra*, p. 311.

rights of parents by passing statutes which compel courts to give deference to the religious element. But some courts evaded the plain requirement of a statute and substituted their own opinions in the matter.

The futility of the type statute, designed to protect the religious feelings of parents, in the face of hostile court action is seen in a Pennsylvania case.

In one case, the usual ante-nuptial promise was signed by a Protestant man about to marry a Catholic.[11] The couple had several children before the wife died. The court found as a fact that the father "at all times showed every intention of carrying out such promise." He had expressed a wish that the children be brought up as Catholics after his death. After the father's death, the Catholic maternal grandaunt contested the appointment of the paternal grandfather, a Protestant, alleging the ante-nuptial promise, the wishes of the father, and particularly the Pennsylvania statute which provided:

> Persons of the same religious persuasion as the parents of the minors shall in all cases be preferred by the court in their appointment as guardians of the persons of such minors.[12]

The court upheld the appointment of the Protestant grandparent. It reasoned that the ante-nuptial promise and later expressed desire of the father were equivalent to bringing him within the term "persuasion," as the term was used in the statute. And it further said that, even if it should so decide that the father's conduct did bring him under the statutory meaning of "persuasion," yet the statute was not mandatory, and that the court approved the award of custody to the Protestant grandparent. The court said that the case "presented squarely" the question whether the provisions of the statute compelled the appointment of a Catholic in view of the existence of the ante-nuptial agreement. It decided the ques-

[11] *In re* Butcher's Guardianship, 226 Pa. 479; 109 At. Rep. 683 (1920).

[12] Pennsylvania: Fiduciaries Act of June 7, 1917 (P. L. 447), Sec. 59 (b).

tion in the negative. Apparently no fault was found with the home of the Catholic grandparent. The material advantages, however, lay with the Protestant grandfather. The decision deserves sharpest criticism. The mandatory words in the statute "shall in all cases be preferred," fairly construed with reference to the object of the statute, could only lead in this case to an award of custody of the children to the Catholic grandparent. The religion of one parent, and the sincere and expressed wish of the other, would then be fulfilled. The decision does violence to the fair construction of the statute. This is a situation where the thought process of the judge is accurately portrayed by a brilliant author and jurist in the following passages: [13]

He (the judge) must balance all his ingredients, his philosophy, his logic, his analogies, his history, his customs, his sense of right and all the rest, and adding a little here and taking out a little there, must determine, as wisely as he can, which weight will tip the scales.

And in addition to

the forces of which judges avowedly avail to shape the form and content of their judgments. . . . Deep below consciousness are other forces, the likes and the dislikes, the predilections and the prejudices, the complex of instincts and emotions and convictions, which make a man whether he be litigant or judge.

It is submitted that the specific element of religious training as a factor in the child's bringing-up should not be left to the individual discretion of each judge. There should exist a distinct presumption in favor of the religious belief of the parents which should not be controlled short of positive harm, if carried out, to the welfare of the child. It is too easy for the courts to swing over into the fixed idea that the child is simply a creature of the state rather than primarily a person of a family, and subject only to the secondary rights of the

[13] Cardozo, *The Nature of the Judicial Process*, pp. 162, 167 (1928).

state. As the law stands now, it is advisable and necessary to impress upon the court the religious status of the child who has been baptized a Catholic in pursuance of the agreement. The English courts have adverted to this important fact that by baptism a status is acquired. The entrance into the Catholic Church is a completed fact, not a prospective or incomplete future membership. It is a complete change and infusion of new spiritual life, and confers graces and helps, and places as well the religious duties of the complete span of life. We are too apt to think that the meaning and significance of the sacrament is known to the court. The vital importance of baptism as the portal of faith and entrance to Church membership should have persuasive force as a most important factor in the court's consideration of the award of custody. The relationship raised between the persons baptized and the sponsors, and the resulting marriage impediment, gives a striking indication of the meaning of baptism beyond the popular conception.[14]

The difficulty of securing a proper and uniform appreciation of the religious element in all these cases is apparent. In order to clear up this uncertain situation, where the same courts decided custody differently in situations closely similar to each

[14] *Marriage Legislation in the New Code of Canon Law,* by H. A. Ayrinhac, Chaps. IV-XII—Spiritual Relationships—A. Origin of the Impediment, pp. 182-183.

Baptism being a new birth, Christians, from the beginning, looked upon those from whom they had received that sacrament as spiritual parents. This spiritual paternity was little by little extended to the sponsors and to those who had assisted in the preparation of the catechumens; then to the ministers and sponsors in the sacrament of Confirmation, which completes Baptism; and also, according to some, to the minister of the sacrament of Penance. This was the *paternitas* and *maternitas spiritualis,* to which was added the *compaternitas* or *commaternitas*; direct or indirect, i. e. the spiritual relationship between the sponsors and the parents of the baptized person or between the baptized person and the husband or wife of the sponsor; then the *confraternitas* or relationship between the baptized person and the children of the spiritual father or mother. Once those relationships were admitted, it was natural that they should be considered as impediments to marriage.

other, some states have passed statutes. These have been passed in an attempt to remove the confusion and to give a guiding principle to courts when considering the religious element in "best welfare" when awarding custody. These statutes and cases decided under them deserve attention and will be considered in the following chapter: "Statutes, present and future."

CHAPTER VII

STATUTES: PRESENT AND FUTURE

WHILE all courts have admitted the existence of some right in the parents whether living or deceased to control the religious up-bringing of their children, these same courts have been at complete variance as to the extent of the right. Some of the courts have evaded the question and rested their decisions upon other considerations. Others have attempted to evaluate the right and to appraise religious membership and training as one of the factors influencing the court in the award of custody of children. But the attempts have failed and have resulted only in a body of ambiguous and even contradictory decisions. The problem of custody arises much more often with the natural growth of population and increased death rate, the urban movement, and the spread of the divorce evil. And it has become further complicated in probation, divorce, abandonment, and separation proceedings, and juvenile criminal cases, as well as in the ordinary petitions for guardianship before probate and chancery courts where one or both parents have died. Many states have attempted to protect this right of the parents, and to bring some uniformity and order out of confusion, by the enactment of statutes. An examination of them reveals no uniformity in provisions or even purpose. These statutes have been passed by some thirty states. Some states dealt with the problem directly by express statutes, while others attempted to achieve the same end indirectly through regulations of departments such as the child welfare division. Some statutes are merely negative, prohibiting distinctions in the care of children because of religion;[1] others are positive in their provision, requiring respect for the particular religious belief. In most of the statutes the term "commitment" is used to describe the proceeding governed by the proposition.[2]

[1] Indiana

1926 Burns Ann. Stat., Sec. 4320.

Orphan Asylum — Distinction as to nativity, religious, or political associations or connections prohibited.

[2] Arizona

1928 Revised Code, Chap. 40, Sec. 1937.

The court, in making orders for the commitment or adoption of children, shall place them, as far as possible, in the care and custody of persons having the same religious belief.

Arkansas

1921 Digest of Statutes, Chap. 90, Sec. 5774—Adoption.

Religious belief—The court in committing children shall place them as far as practicable in the care and custody of some individual holding the same religious belief as the parent of said child or with some association which is controlled by persons of like religious faith of the parents of said child.

Colorado

1921 Statutes, Chap. 19, No. 608, Sec. 7.

"....If the state home cannot provide for any child committed to it with voluntary adoption within six months, then it must provide as far as possible for the boarding-out of such child in some suitable family home, until such time as it may be adopted or shall have reached the age of 16 years. Religious beliefs of the family from which the child came must be respected."

Connecticut

1930 General Statutes Rev. Title 14, Chap. 95, Sec. 1867.

Religious faith of parents of child to be respected in commitment.

Georgia

1926 General Code—Penal Code, Art. XI, Sec. 900 (34).

Religious belief of parent in committing child is respected.

Illinois

1929 Cahill Rev. Statutes, Chap. 23, Parag. 340, Sec. 17, p. 248.

The court in committing children shall place them as far as practicable in the care and custody of some individual holding the same religious belief as the parents of said child, or with some association which is controlled by persons of like religious faith of the parents of said child.

Iowa

1931 Code, Chap. 180, Sec. 3640.

The court in committing children shall place them as far as practicable in the care and custody of some individual holding the same religious belief as the parents of said child, or with some institution which is controlled by persons of like religious faith with the parents of said child.

Kentucky

1930 Kentucky Statutes, Sec. 331 E —14. Commitment.

Religious belief of parents always considered in placing child.

Missouri

1929 Revised Statute, Sec. 392 (Guardians).

A minor shall not be committed to the guardianship of a person of religious persuasion different from that of the parents, or of the surviving parent of the minor, if another suitable person can be procured, unless the minor being of proper age should so choose. (R. S. 1919, parag. 388). See 162 S. W. 119, and 45 Mo. 602; 16 Mo. App. 159.

Nebraska

1929 Compiled Statutes, Secs. 43-216.

The court in committing children under the provisions of this article, shall place them as far as practicable in the care and custody of some individual holding the same religious belief as the parents of said child, or with some association which is controlled by persons of like religious faith of the parents of the said child.

Nevada

1929 Compiled Laws, Vol. I, Sec. 1030.

The court in committing children shall place them as far as practicable in the care and custody of some individual holding the same religious belief as the parents of the said child, or with some association or institution which is controlled by persons of like religious faith of the parents of the said child.

New Hampshire

1926 Public Laws, Chap. 110, Sec. 16.

The religious preference of the parents shall be respected in committals of children to individuals, associations, etc.

New York

1930 Cahill Cons. Law, Chap. 67, p. 2703, Art. 3, Sec. 26.

Religion of custodial persons and agencies. Commitment must be made to institutions, persons or associations other than one controlled by the state or a subdivision thereof, or the placement of a child in a family, or home, or in the custody of a person other than that of its parents or in guardianship or adoption out, according to the religious faith of the child, when practicable. This provision shall be interpreted literally.

Ibidem, Chap. 56, p. 2145, Sec. 302.

Wherever a child is committed to any agency, association, corporation, institution or society other than an institution supported and controlled by the state or a subdivision thereof, such commitment shall be made when practicable to an authorized agency under the control of persons of the same religious faith as that of the child.

Ohio

1930 Throckmorton's Ann. Code, Chap. 8, Sec. 1679.

Religious belief — The judge in committing children shall place them, so far as practicable, in the care and custody of an individual holding the same religious belief as such child or its parents, or with some association which is controlled by persons of like religious faith as such child or parent.

Pennsylvania

1930 Purdon's, Title 11, Sec. 146.

The court, in making all orders for the commitment of children, shall place them, as far as possible, in care and custody of persons having the same religious belief as the parents of the child, or with some association which is controlled by persons of such religious belief, etc.

South Dakota

1929 Comp. Laws, Chap. 4, Art. 2, Sec. 9993.

The court in committing the child shall place such child in the care and custody of some individual of like religious faith or with an association which is controlled by persons of like religious faith as the parents of such child.

West Virginia

1931 Official Code, Chap. 49, Art. 4, Sec. 3.

The court in committing any child shall place such child, as far as practicable, in the care and custody of some individual holding the same religious belief as the parents or relatives of such child.

In a few, the much broader term "custody" is used.[3]

[3] Arizona

1928 Revised Code, Chap. 40, Sec. 1937, *supra.*

Delaware

1915 Revised Code, Chap. 116, No. 3841, Sec. 26.

. . . and in all cases where it can be properly done, the child shall be placed in an approved family home, with people of the same religious belief if this is reasonably possible.

Illinois

1929 Cahill Rev. Statutes, Chap. 23, Parag. 340, Sec. 17, *supra.*

Nebraska

1929 Compiled Statutes, Secs. 43-216, *supra.*

Nevada

1929 Compiled Laws, Vol. I, Sec. 1030, *supra.*

New York

1930 Cahill Cons. Law, Chap. 67, p. 2703, Art. 3, Sec. 26, *supra.*

North Carolina

1931 Code, Art. 2 Chap. 90, Sec. 5053.

Religious preference of parent of child respected in selecting a custodial agency.

Ohio

1930 Throckmorton's Ann. Code, Chap. 8, Sec. 1679, *supra.*

Pennsylvania

1930 Purdon's Pennsylvania Statutes.

Title 48 Marriage, Chap. II, Sec. 91, Note 4.

Mother to have same power and control over minor child as father.

Ibidem, Sec. 92—Judge to decide dispute as to children's custody.

Ibidem, Title 11, Sec. 146.

South Dakota

1929 Comp. Laws, Chap. 4, Art. 2, Sec. 9993, *supra.*

West Virginia

1931 Official Code, Chap. 49, Art. 4, Sec. 3, *supra.*

Several require that the religious belief is to be "respected." [4]

[4] Colorado

1921 Statutes, Chap. 19, No. 608, Sec. 7, *supra.*

Connecticut

1930 Gen. Statutes Revised, Chap. 95, Sec. 1867, *supra.*

Georgia

1926 Gen. Code, Penal Code, Art. XI, Sec. 900 (34), *supra.*

Massachusetts

1921 Gen. Laws, Chap. 119, Sec. 40.

Religious beliefs of parents of child respected. See also 1931 Acts and 1 Resolves, Chap. 342.

Minnesota

1927 Mason's Minnesota Statutes, Chap. 73 A, Sec. 8655.

Religious beliefs of parents respected as to placement of children.

Missouri

1929 Rev. Statutes, Sec. 14154.

Religious faith of parents of child to be respected.

Montana

1921 Rev. Code, Sec. 12291.

Religious beliefs of parents respected in child placement.

New Hampshire

1926 Public Laws, Chap. 110, Sec. 16, *supra.*

New Jersey

1925 Cum. Supp., 53-215°.

Religious beliefs of parents of child in placement respected. Where conditions have changed so that it is for the best interest of the child that it be with its parents, court may so order.

North Carolina
1931 Code, Art. 2, Chap. 90, Sec. 5053, *supra.*
South Carolina
1923 Public Acts, p. 216, Sec. 15.
The religious faith of the parents shall be respected when placed out.

And in these the greater number add the religious belief of the parents. New York and Maryland provide by statute that the religion referred to shall be that of the child.[5] The laws again differ in regard to the consideration to be given the religious preference. As has been pointed out, one type of statute requires "respect";[6] another requires the placing in a home having "suitable religious advantage";[7] another gives "prefer-

[5] Maryland
1927, Chap. 689—(Amending Sec. 3 of Art. 4 of the Ann. Code of Maryland—title, "Almshouses and Trustees of the Poor", be repealed and re-enacted with amendments read.) Section 3. The county commissioners—Trustees of the Poor shall place all such children with a family, institution or agency duly authorized as aforesaid under the control of a person or persons of the same religious faith or persuasion as the child.
New York
1930 Cahill Cons. Law, Chap. 67, p. 2703, Art. 3, Sec. 26, *supra.*
Ibidem, Chap. 56, p. 2145, Sec. 302, *supra.*
Ohio
1930 Throckmorton's Ann. Code, Chap. 8, Sec. 1679, *supra.*
Tennessee
1932 Code, Chap. 14, 4735 (4436a24).
All children placed out in private families shall be, as far as it is practicable, located with those of the same religious faith as that held by the children themselves, or their parents.
Wyoming
1920 Comp. Statutes, Chap. 246, Sec. 3903, Sub-sec. 2.
All children placed out in private families shall be, as far as it is practicable, located with those of the same religious faith as that held by the children themselves or the parents.

[6] See note 56, *supra.*

[7] Delaware
1915 Rev. Code, Chap. 116, No. 3841, Sec. 26, *supra.*
Kansas
1923 Rev. Statute, Secs. 38-305, duty.—Child placement.
It shall be the duty of the institution, etc. . . . Said society is au-

ence" to prospective guardians of the same faith.[8] And the court is to follow the statutory provision "when practicable,"[9] or in one state "in all cases."[10] The confusion is apparent.

thorized to secure for such children legal adoption in such families . . . suitable religious advantages.

[8] New Hampshire
1926 Public Laws, Chap. 110, Sec. 16, *supra.*
North Carolina
1931 Code, Art. 2, Chap. 90, Sec. 5053, *supra.*
Pennsylvania
Purdon's Digest, 13th ed., 1084, title 20, Vol. 20.
Now appears as parag. 1022—Preferment of Religious Faith (re-enacted 1917).
Persons of the same religious persuasion as the parents of the minors shall in all cases be preferred by the court in their appointment as guardians of the persons of such minors.

[9] Arkansas
1921 Digest of the Statutes, Chap. 90, Sec. 5774, *supra.*
Illinois
1929 Cahill Rev. Statutes, Chap. 23, parag. 340, Sec. 17, p. 284, *supra.*
Iowa
1927 Code, Chap. 180, Sec. 3640, *supra.*
Nebraska
1929 Comp. Statutes, Secs. 43-216, *supra.*
Nevada
1929 Comp. Laws, Vol. I, Sec. 1030, *supra.*
New York
1930 Cahill Cons. Law, Chap. 67, p. 2703, Art. 3, Sec. 26, *supra.*
1930 Cahill Cons. Law, Chap. 56, p. 2145, Sec. 302, *supra.*
Ohio
1930 Throckmorton's Ann. Code, Chap. 8, Sec. 1679, *supra.*
Tennessee
1932 Code, Chap. 14, Sec. 4735 (4436a24), *supra.*
West Virginia
1931 Official Code, Chap. 49, Art. 4, Sec. 3, *supra.*
Wyoming
1920 Comp. Statutes, Chap. 246, Sec. 3903, Sub-sec. 2, *supra.*

[10] Massachusetts
General Laws of 1921, Chap. 119, Sec. 40.

No parents, or surviving parents, of any minor child in the care or under the supervision of the department, or any state department, or of any State Board of Trustees, shall be denied the request of any child of theirs to the free exercise of the religious belief of his parents and the liberty of worshipping God according to the religion which

Parents' rights are violated; courts have been unnecessarily burdened and worried. The following statute takes into account the situation when parents are of different religious beliefs:

> . . . It shall be the duty of the board of charities and probation whenever possible to place out dependent children of the state in institutions or homes where the aforesaid dependent children shall be brought up in the religion of their parents, *or in case the parents are of different religious faith but have agreed upon bringing up their children in any particular faith, the board shall abide by that agreement.*[11]

Many states are at present working upon revisions and consolidations of their statutes. All states in the near future will probably undertake such compilations. It is submitted that the enactment of a statute, such as the following, would simplify and clarify the situation, protect parent's rights, and give courts a uniform and reasonable guide:

> Courts in any proceeding involving custody of children shall so far as practicable place said children under the control of persons of the same religious belief as the parents, if said parents are of the same religious belief; or in accordance with any hitherto existing agreement, if said parents are of different religious beliefs.

In this connexion, it seems advisable to suggest the following form of ante-nuptial agreement as a clear direct statement, incorporating the promises required by Canon Law, and fulfiling the requirements of the civil law of contracts. All agreements should be in writing upon a single form signed by both parties. The agreement should take the form of mutual prom-

> his parents professed, if they are both deceased; and no minor child in the care or under the supervision of the department, or of any state department, or State Board of Trustees, shall be denied the free exercise of the religion of his parents, or of his surviving parent, or of his parents if they are both deceased, nor the liberty of worshipping God according to the religion of his parents whether living or deceased.

[11] Vermont, 1919 Public Acts, p. 216, No. 207, Sec. 1. (Italics inserted.)

ises given by each party directly to the other in consideration of marriage and not extended to include any other parties. From a legal point of view this is essential. It is also undesirable to complicate the agreement with additional provisions beyond the necessary requirements by Canon Law. It is true of this, as of all other contracts, that surplusage tends to complicate and to confuse the issue in question. To illustrate, the added phrase " upon my honor " would be singled out at once as an expression in contradistinction to a contractual and legally binding obligation. Other similar phrases expose the agreement to like criticism.[12] The recommended form is as follows:

[12] It seems to the writer that such expressions as " The non-Catholic party understands that this is an indissoluble union ", and " No other ceremony will be performed before a civil magistrate ", and other similar provisions relative to witnesses, etc., can be made clear apart from the agreement. Added provisions in the suggested form or even in a separate form may expose the whole agreement to legal attack.

—————————— (Date)

—————————— (Town)

—————————— (County)

—————————— (State)

We, ———— ———— of ———— in the county of ————, and state of ————, and ————, ———— of ————, in the county of ———— and state of ————, hereby mutually promise each other that all the children of our marriage shall be baptized and brought up solely in the Roman Catholic religion.

I, the said ———— ————, hereby promise to remove any danger to, or hindrance to, the Catholic faith, morals or religious practice of the said ———— ————.

Each of us enters this agreement with full knowledge of the meaning of the religious belief of, and its significance to the said ———— ————, the Catholic party. And each of us further understands that the execution of this agreement and the promises therein contained are made in contemplation of and in consideration for the consent, marriage and consequent change of status of the said Catholic party ———— ————.

These promises and covenants herein contained shall inure to and be binding on our respective heirs, next of kin, administrators, executors, and/or subsequent guardians and their successors.

In witness whereof we have hereunto affixed our hands and seals at ———— this ———— day of ————.

———————— (Seal)

———————— (Seal)

Witness:

1. ————————

2. ————————

(Pastor, Assistant)

The agreement should be executed, if possible, a reasonable time before the ceremony. Each party should be given a copy, and one retained in the files of the rectory, and another forwarded to the chancery of the diocese. It seems the better practice to have at least one witness, who is a lay person, in addition to the clerical witness. A supplementary record of the dates of religious instruction of the non-Catholic party would be also helpful. These formalities would insure the availability of the agreement at a subsequent time and remove possible doubts as to the execution of the agreement and the meaning of its terms.

In review the present statutes compel the conclusion in the mind of any fair reader that the situation is unnecessarily confused and leads easily into the deprivation of rights of parents to control the religious upbringing of the children. The courts, faced with contradictory decisions, are unnecessarily handicapped in their judicial findings and orders relating to the custody of children. The rights of parents can be protected and courts relieved of embarrassment by the passage of such a statute as has been outlined. Finally, to conform with such simplification, the form of the ante-nuptial promises has been suggested as one in which the agreement would fulfill the requirements of Canon Law as well as the requirements of the civil law of contracts.

CHAPTER VIII

Public Policy

Any discussion concerning the legal effect of ante-nuptial promises would lack completeness without reference to "public policy." For opponents may urge the vague but high-sounding objection that the agreement is "against public policy." Just what "public policy" is, and precisely how this contract might offend against it, would probably be left to conjecture. But it might be useful to anticipate such possible arguments. In one or two of the English decisions where this objection was raised the court explained its meaning. Compelling a parent through court action to set aside money to be used in religious training in a sect to which he is opposed was said to be against public policy. As was indicated above, this objection has been repeated. It could hardly be argued with any seriousness now; for religious upbringing in the United States today would not require the court to sequester any particular funds. That must be obvious. Another objection which might be raised along this line would be that the enforcement of the agreement would tend to disturb the harmony of the family household. This may be answered with the sound observations of a law professor writing upon the subject of tort action between husband and wife to the effect that "when suits are brought, there is not much domestic tranquility left to be disturbed." [1] The objection seems to disregard the fact that the Catholic party has changed his or her status in reliance upon the ante-nuptial agreement and the further fact that the non-Catholic has made the agreement with reference to the

[1] W. E. McCurdy, "Torts Between Persons in Domestic Relations", 43 *Harv. L. Rev.*, 1930, 1052 (1930).

full import of the meaning of marriage and parent-bond to the Catholic party. It is well to remember all through the discussion on "public policy" the remarks of a Justice of the United States Supreme Court:

> In order to enter into most of the relations of life people have to give up some of their constitutional rights. If a man makes a contract he gives up the constitutional right that previously he had to be free from the hamper that he puts upon himself.[2]

Closely akin to the above objections is that which stresses the practical difficulty of courts ordering a child to be brought up in a religion different from that of the person in whose custody the child is placed. It may be well to repeat here a statement made earlier that legal enforcement of the antenuptial agreement does not necessarily involve the question of custody. While placing children in the custody of parties of a different religion is not an ideal situation, it has not prevented courts from giving such orders. Both English[3] and American[4] courts have affirmatively ordered that the child be brought up in a religion different from that of one or both guardians. The particularity of the court's order in regard to such training has

[2] Mr. J. Holmes, in dissenting in Power Mfg. Co. *v.* Saunders, 274 U. S. 490, 497 (1927).

[3] English:

Austin *v.* Austin, 4 De Gex. Jones & Smith Rep. 716 (1865). The husband died a Catholic. The children were committed to the custody of the mother with directions that they should be raised Catholics.

[4] American:

In re Lamb's Estate, 139 N. Y. Supp., 685 (1912)—the child was placed in the custody of a Protestant aunt, but a Catholic woman was named co-guardian to provide for Catholic education.

In re Mancini, 151 N. Y. Supp., 387; 89 Misc. Rep., 83 (1915)—Custody of the child was given to a Protestant minister with directions to have it educated in a Catholic residential institution.

People *v.* Lackey, 248 N. Y. Supp., 560; 139 Misc. Rep., 42 (1930)—The court placed the children with a Protestant and appointed a Catholic priest co-guardian of them.

not proved any obstacle to the granting of relief.[5] The courts of equity have framed a scheme for religious education in such circumstances.

It is idle to inject into this discussion any extreme cases in which the enforcing of alleged religious views of a parent would subject the child to moral contamination or physical suffering. It should be apparent that in those cases the divine, natural, and civil law unite to assert the right of the child. As the Holy Father has said:

It also belongs to the State to protect the rights of the child itself when the parents are found wanting either physically or morally in this respect, whether by default, incapacity or misconduct, since, as has been shown, their right to educate is not an absolute and despotic one, but dependent on the natural and divine law, and therefore subject alike to the authority and jurisdiction of the Church, and to the vigilance and administrative care of the State in view of the common good. Besides, the family is not a perfect society, that is, it has not in itself all the means necessary for its full development. In such cases, exceptional no doubt, the State does not put itself in the place of the family, but merely supplies deficiencies, and provides suitable means, always in conformity with the natural rights of the child and the supernatural rights of the Church.[6]

Perhaps all of these objections under "public policy" have become part of the modern vogue to evade the question of the enforcement of any religious right which has arisen in legal proceedings, and the excuse is often the convenient exit of "public policy." How far such an attitude is the concomitant of the spreading wish to submerge religion need not be discussed here. Suffice it to say, that the question of the legal enforce-

[5] Austin *v.* Austin, *supra.*

[6] Pope Pius XI, *The Christian Education of Youth*, p. 17 (N. C. W. C., 1930).

ability of the ante-nuptial agreement cannot be disposed of so lightly.[7]

One who denies the legal enforceability of the ante-nuptial agreement on the purported ground that it is against "public policy" should be forced to define "public policy" and state the specific way in which the contract offends against it. In the legal sense, "public policy" is found to have a restricted meaning, and contracts against public policy have even a much narrower definition. It applies for the most part to contracts to commit criminal or immoral acts. Story, an eminent authority on contracts, has said of public policy:

> . . . It has never been defined by the courts, but has been left loose and free of definition, in the same manner as fraud. . . . This rule may, however, be safely laid down, that whenever any contract conflicts with the morals of the time, and contravenes any established interest of society, it is void, as being against public policy.[8]

A leading English case further illustrates this narrow meaning. In this case the vendor of a patent contracted to assign to the plaintiff all future patent rights of a like nature which the defendant might hereafter acquire. The defendant contended that he could not be compelled to do so on the ground

[7] A contract against "public policy", as one famous American law professor has replied: "Public policy and estoppel—the gold-dust twins of the law, upon whose shoulders fall the work of furnishing a plausible reason to a lazy legal intellect."

[8] Story: Contracts (2 ed.), Sec. 546, p. 480. *Cf.* also Mr. Justice Holmes, in Otis *v.* Parker, 187 U. S. 606, 608, 609 (1903): "While the courts must exercise a judgment of their own, it by no means is true that every law is void which may seem to the judges who pass upon it excessive, unsuited to its ostensible end, or based upon conceptions of morality with which they disagree. Considerable latitude must be allowed for differences of view as well as for possible peculiar conditions which this Court can know but imperfectly, if at all. Otherwise a constitution, instead of embodying only relatively fundamental rules of right, as generally understood by all English-speaking communities, would become the partisan of a particular set of ethical or economic opinions, which by no means are held *semper, ubique et ab omnibus. . . .*"

that such an agreement was opposed to public policy. The court, however, upheld the agreement. Sir George Jessel, M. R., said in the opinion:

> It must not be forgotten that you are not to extend arbitrarily those rules which say that a given contract is void as being against public policy, because if there is one thing which more than another public policy requires it is that men of full age and competent understanding shall have the utmost liberty of contracting, and that their contracts when entered into freely and voluntarily shall be held sacred and shall be enforced by Courts of Justice. Therefore, you have this paramount public policy to consider—that you are not lightly to interfere with this freedom of contract. Now, there is no doubt public policy may say that a contract to commit a crime, or a contract to give a reward to another to commit a crime, is necessarily void. The decisions have gone further, and contracts to commit an immoral offence or to induce another to do something against the rules of morality, though far more indefinite than the previous class, have always been held to be void. I should be sorry to extend the doctrine much further.[9]

The United States Supreme Court has likewise construed contracts against public policy very narrowly: In Baltimore & Ohio Railway Co. *v.* Voight. The Express Company contracted with the Railroad Company to hold the latter harmless in case of injury to any of the express personnel while using the cars and rails of the Railway Company. And in addition to entering employment with such condition, Voight separately contracted with the Express Company to hold them harmless in case of personal injury to himself. Voight was injured and sued the Railway Company. He contended that the contracts in question were void as against public policy. The court held that Voight was in no sense a passenger of the Railroad Company; that he was not constrained to enter into the contract but did so freely and seeking benefit to himself, and the contract

[9] Printing and Numerical Registering Co. *v.* Sampson, 19 L. R. Equity 462, 465 (1875).

could not be said to contravene public policy. Mr. Justice Shiras said in that regard:

> At the same time it must not be forgotten that the right to private contract is no small part of the liberty of the citizen, and that the usual and most important function of courts of justice is rather to maintain and enforce contracts, than to enable parties thereto to escape from their obligation on the pretext of public policy, unless it clearly appear that they contravene public right or the public welfare.[10]

The question may be met squarely. There is no need of evasion. Is an ante-nuptial agreement executed by a Catholic and a non-Catholic, the basis upon which a Catholic changes irrevocably his or her status within whose ambit is included all present and future and eternal happiness, to be tossed over by simple resort to the magniloquent phrase—"against public policy"? Is religious conviction in America to be reduced to the legal standing of a mere dilettante taste, phantom, hobby or what-you-will, or is it to still retain its prime and robust meaning which it had for the founders of our nation—a priceless possession with real objective value containing the very essence, meaning and explanation of life? If this is a Christian nation, does membership in the Church of pioneer Christianity have a legal sanction? Or have we forgotten in the busy whirl and lost heart in the face of the vigorous attack upon all religion? It will thus be seen that the objections against the legal enforcement of ante-nuptial promises on the ground of public policy are vague and flimsy. The protection of the courts for this contract is neither state aid nor protection of a church as such. It is the request of a fundamental right of a citizen: the law's protection of a legal contract. That protection may be the more reasonably demanded because this is a contract in regard to the Christian religion.

[10] Baltimore & Ohio Ry. Co. *v.* Voight, 176 U. S. 498, 505 (1900).

Mr. Justice Sutherland has said in a recent case before the United States Supreme Court: " We are a Christian people," [11] citing a noted case decided by the same court.[12] The latter case presents a long review of authorities which supported the proposition. Starting with the very earliest indication in the commission to Christopher Columbus, there are found the words: " It is hoped that by God's assistance some of the continents and islands in the oceans will be discovered." [13] Mr. Justice Brewer continued to quote freely from many documents which consistently prove the thesis. References are made to the first colonial grant to Sir Walter Raleigh in 1584,[14] the first charters to Virginia granted by King James I in 1606, and the subsequent charters of the same colony, to the celebrated compact made by the Pilgrims in the Mayflower in 1620.[15] The fundamental orders of Connecticut under which the provisional government was instituted in 1638,[16] and the charter of privileges granted by William Penn to the province of Pennsylvania in 1701.[17] In all of these charters one of the prime purposes is declared to be the establishment of the Christian religion.

In the charter of privileges granted by William Penn to the province of Pennsylvania in 1701, it is recited; and, coming nearer to the present time, the Declaration of Independence recognizes the presence of the Divine in human affairs. If we examine the constitutions of the various States we find in them a constant recognition of religious obligations. Every constitution of everyone of the forty-eight States contains language

[11] United States *v.* MacIntosh, 283 U. S. 605, 625 (1930).

[12] Holy Trinity Church *v.* United States, 143 U. S. 457, 465 (1892).

[13] Holy Trinity Church *v.* United States, 143 U. S. 457, 465 (1892).

[14] *Ibidem,* p. 466.

[15] *Ibidem,* p. 466.

[16] *Ibidem,* p. 466.

[17] *Ibidem,* p. 467.

which either directly or by clear implication recognizes a profound reverence for religion and an assumption that its influence in all human affairs is essential to the well-being of the community.[18]

The honorable Justice reviews the requirements and the form of the oaths required in various states, with particular reference to the invocation of Divine Help, and concludes:

If we pass beyond these matters to a view of American life as expressed by its laws, its business, its customs and its society, we find everywhere a clear recognition of the same truth. Among other matters note the following: The form of oath universally prevailing, concluding with an appeal to the Almighty; the custom of opening sessions of all deliberative bodies and most conventions with prayer; the prefatory words of all wills, "In the name of God, amen"; the laws respecting the observance of the Sabbath, with the general cessation of all secular business, and the closing of courts, legislatures, and other similar public assemblies on that day; the churches and church organizations which abound in every city, town, and hamlet: the multitude of charitable organizations existing everywhere under Christian auspices; the gigantic missionary associations, with general support, and aiming to establish Christian missions in every quarter of the globe. These, and many other matters which might be noticed add a volume of unofficial declarations to the mass of organic utterances that this is a Christian nation.[19]

[18] *Ibidem*, p. 468.

[19] *Ibidem*, p. 471.

CHAPTER IX

Conclusion

To some it may appear to be a rash undertaking to have attempted an accurate investigation of the legal considerations determining the present legal effect of ante-nuptial promises. It may seem bolder still to attempt to appraise the present and future status of the ante-nuptial agreement. But the hazard is well ventured if it succeeds in exposing the weak foundations of an apparent legal barrier built upon a foundation of historical prejudice and mistaken precedents uncritically accepted in some of our English and American courts. It is well to remember that this English prejudice had had a real legal significance, rendering such an agreement void as part of a drastic and barbarous group of laws making the teaching or practicing of the Catholic religion punishable even by death.[1]

[1] "8 Ann., c. 3, parag. 16. A papist teaching publicly or privately, or intertained as an usher to a protestant schoolmaster, to be esteemed a popish regular clergyman convict, and suffer all the pains inflicted upon such, that is, 1st. to be imprisoned in the common gaol; 2d. to be transported; 3d. if he return to his friends and native land, to suffer as a traitor: the following is his judgment.

"1st. To be dragged along the ground to the place of execution; 2d. to be hanged by the neck; 3d. to have his entrails taken out and burned while he is yet alive; 4th. his head to be cut off; 5th. that his body be quartered or divided into four parts; 6th. that his head and quarters be at the pleasure of the Queen.

"The legal consequences of this judgment are, attainder, corruption of blood, annihilation of all inheritable powers, from his ancestors and to his heirs. . . .

". . . A protestant permitting a child under fourteen to be educated a papist, to suffer as a papist."—The Catholic Question in America. Decided at the Court of Gen. Sessions, City of New York, with the unanimous arguments of counsel. Reported by William Sampson (New York: E. Gillespy, 1813), p. 125.

Once this obstacle to a proper judicial appraisal is removed, courts can view the question unhampered by pre-judgments. While it is of course undesirable to exaggerate the influence of prejudice, it is nevertheless necessary to realize the fact of its presence in the past and the possibility of its future effect. The historical attitude of the Church and the object of the present Decree should be explained fully. No idea is more remote from the mind of the Church than that the requirement of the execution of the agreement is a means of forcing people into her fold. On the contrary, she is unalterably opposed to Catholics marrying non-Catholics. Her decrees, Canon Law, writings, and teachings—all give clear proof of her attitude. The reason is plain and practical. Entrusted by Christ with the truth, she cannot tamper with it; she must preserve the true faith for her children and their offspring. Enriched with the human experience of twenty centuries, she knows, as all fair and intelligent men must admit, that in such marriages:

> . . . When minds do not agree as to the observance of religion, it is scarcely possible to hope for agreement in other things. Other reasons also proving that persons should turn with dread from such marriages are chiefly . . . that they are a hindrance to the proper education of the children.[2]

This teaching has been emphasized in a recent encyclical by the present Pontiff. In his admonition against mixed marriages, he states once more the valid reasoning of the Church's position:

> Assuredly, also, will there be wanting that close union of spirit which, as it is the sign and mark of the Church of Christ, so also should be the sign of Christian wedlock, its glory and adornment. For where there exists diversity of mind, truth and feeling, the bond of union of mind and heart is wont to be broken, or at least weakened. From this comes the danger lest the love of man and

[2] *Great Encyclical Letters of Leo XIII*, Christian Marriage, p. 81.

wife grow cold and the peace and happiness of family life, resting as it does on the union of hearts, be destroyed.[8]

However, the Church allows her ministers to officiate in the event that a grave cause exists, that the agreement has been executed, and when the pastor is morally certain that it will be observed.

To the non-Catholic a civil marriage is available. But with a full understanding of the consequences he or she chooses to enter the agreement with a person of the Catholic faith in a Catholic ceremony; and, having executed the agreement, common honesty demands its observance. Tested by accepted legal criteria, it is submitted that the agreement has the essential elements of a contract and is similar to other ante-nuptial contracts the legal force of which has never been doubted. The agreement is made with direct reference to the religious belief of the Catholic, particularly as it involves marriage, bearing children as the primary end of matrimony, and the consequent duties of parenthood. As such it gives the Catholic party an added right of personality, one of a group of rights of personality, to which modern courts of equity are steadily extending their protection. In the situation where one or both parents are dead, we have seen a large number of states in a variety of statutes have attempted to give legal effect to the religious belief of the parents and the religious status of the child. However confusing and ineffectual the result today, the purpose of the state legislation could be secured and courts relieved of difficulty by the passage of the suggested statute. The framing of the proposed agreement has also been suggested for the purpose of simplification, rather than correction, of existing Chancery forms. It is submitted that objections to the legal enforceability have been treated and effectually answered. Of course, it is too much to hope that all objections will be silenced. Objec-

[8] Pope Pius XI: Present "Encylical on Marriage" (*Casti Connubii*), 31 Dec., 1930.

tions based upon difficulties, real and fanciful, can be raised against the enforcement of every legal right. Too often the critic will be inclined to ignore the plain fact that this is an agreement, voluntarily executed by a person fully appraised of its meaning and aware that, upon the expectancy of its fulfillment, the Catholic party irrevocably changes status, and further assumes serious and holy duties upon the fulfillment of which will depend (to that individual) present and eternal happiness.

As to predictions, obviously the writer cannot guarantee that cases will always be well considered by able judges. But apart from that rare situation, the ante-nuptial agreement should find a proper judicial appraisal in American courts which proceed beyond out-moded historical misinterpretations and which advance with the needs of the present and future and are alive to the spirit of progress in the law. The writer submits this analysis of the legal effect of ante-nuptial promises in mixed marriage with the confidence that a court or legislature which aims to see through merely artificial or apparent barriers will perceive the true legal nature of the ante-nuptial agreement. Such courts and legislatures, recognizing the right of personality which accrues to the Catholic party and conscious of inherent power to protect such a claim, will proceed to make the legal enforceability of ante-nuptial promises a reality in accordance with the demands of plain justice and the spirit of American tradition.

TABLE OF CASES

ENGLISH CASES

AMERICAN CASES.

AMERICAN STATUTES.

ENGLISH STATUTES.

Universitas Catholica Americae

Washingtonii, D. C.

FACULTAS JURIS CANONICI

1934

No. 91

DEUS LUX MEA

TITULI

QUOS

AD DOCTORATUS GRADUM

IN

JURE CANONICO

APUD UNIVERSITATEM CATHOLICAM AMERICAE

CONSEQUENDUM

PUBLICE PROPUGNABIT

ROBERTUS JACOBUS WHITE

SACERDOS DIOECESIS

PORTLANDENSIS

JURIS CANONICI LICENTIATUS

HORA XI A.M., DIE XXXI MAII MCMXXXIV

TITULI

IN IURE CANONICO

I.	De Dissertatione.		
II.	De Historia Iuris Canonici.		
III.	Canones	1-7	De Ambitu Codicis.
IV.	Canones	8-24	De Legibus Ecclesiasticis.
V.	Canones	25-30	De Consuetudine.
VI.	Canones	31-35	De Temporis Supputatione.
VII.	Canones	36-62	De Rescriptis.
VIII.	Canones	63-79	De Privilegiis.
IX.	Canones	80-86	De Dispensationibus.
X.	Canones	87-107	Generales Notiones de Personis.
XI.	Canones	111-117	De Clericorum Adscriptione Alicui Dioecesi.
XII.	Canones	118-123	De Iuribus et Privilegiis Clericorum.
XIII.	Canones	124-144	De Obligationibus Clericorum.
XIV.	Canones	145-195	De Officiis Ecclesiasticis.
XV.	Canones	196-210	De Potestate Ordinaria et Delegata.
XVI.	Canones	487-498	De Notione Religionis, et de Erectione et Suppressione Religionis, Provincia, Domus.
XVII.	Canones	499-537	De Religionum Regimine.
XVIII.	Canones	538-586	De Admissione in Religionem.
XIX.	Canones	592-631	De Obligationibus et Privilegiis Religiosorum.
XX.	Canones	637-645	De Egressu e Religione.
XXI.	Canones	646-672	De Dimissione Religiosorum.
XXII.	Canones	1012-1018	De Matrimonio in Genere.
XXIII.	Canones	1019-1034	De Iis quae Matrimonii Celebrationi Praemitti Debent.

XXIV.	Canones 1035-1057	De Impedimentis in Genere.
XXV.	Canones 1058-1066	De Impedimentis Impedientibus.
XXVI.	Canones 1067-1080	De Impedimentis Dirimentibus.
XXVII.	Canones 1081-1093	De Consensu Matrimoniali.
XXVIII.	Canones 1552-1568	De Notione Iudici et de Foro Competenti.
XXIX.	Canones 1569-1607	De Variis Tribunalium Gradibus et Speciebus.
XXX.	Canones 1608-1645	De Disciplina in Tribunalibus Servanda.
XXXI.	Canones 1646-1666	De Partibus in Causa.
XXXII.	Canones 1667-1705	De Actionibus et Exceptionibus.
XXXIII.	Canones 1706-1725	De Causae Introductione.
XXXIV.	Canones 1726-1746	De Litis Contestatione, de Litis Instantia, et de Interrogationibus Partibus in Iudicio Faciendis.
XXXV.	Canones 1747-1836	De Probationibus.
XXXVI.	Canones 1837-1857	De Causis Incidentibus.
XXXVII.	Canones 1858-1877	De Processus Publicatione, de Conclusione in Causa, de Causae Discussione, et de Sententia.
XXXVIII.	Canones 1960-1992	De Causis Matrimonialibus.
XXXIX.	Canones 2195-2198	De Natura Delicti eisque Divisione.
XL.	Canones 2199-2211	De Imputabilitate Delicti, de Causis illam Aggravantibus vel Minuentibus, et de Iuridicis Delicti Effectibus.
XLI.	Canones 2212-2213	De Conatu Delicti.
XLII.	Canones 2214-2240	De Poenis in Genere.
XLIII.	Canones 2241-2285	De Poenis Medicinalibus seu de Censuris.
XLIV.	Canones 2286-2305	De Poenis Vindicativis.
XLV.	Canones 2306-2313	De Remediis Poenalibus et Poenitentiis.

ROMAN LAW

XLVI. The periods of Roman Law.
XLVII. Personality.
XLVIII. Wrongs against the Person.
XLIX. Wrongs against Property.
L. Quasi-Delicts.
LI. Patria Potestas.
LII. Res.
LIII. Tutela et Cura.
LIV. Inheritance.
LV. Ownership.

AMERICAN CHURCH CIVIL LAW

LVI. Tax Exemption.
LVII. Trusts.
LVIII. Marriage.
LIX. Christian Burial.
LX. Wills.

BIBLIOGRAPHY

Sources

Ante-Nicene Fathers, 10 vols., Scribner's, New York, 1899.

Acta Apostolicae Sedis (A. A. S.), Rome, 1909.

Codex Iuris Canonici Pii X Pontificis Maximi iussu digestus Benedicti Papae XV auctoritate promulgatus, Rome, 1918.

Codicis Iuris Canonici Fontes, ed. Petri Card. Gasparri, 4 vols., Rome, 1926.

Concilii Plenarii Baltimorensis I (1852), *Acta et Decreta*, Baltimore, 1853.

Concilii Plenarii Baltimorensis II (1866), *Acta et Decreta*, Baltimore, 1868.

Concilii Plenarii Baltimorensis III (1884), *Acta et Decreta*, Baltimore, 1886.

Corpus Scriptorum Ecclesiasticorum Latinorum, Vindobonae, 1866—

Four Great Encyclicals, New York, 1932.

Mansi, J. D., *Sacrorum Conciliorum Nova et Amplissima Collectio*, 51 vols., Florence, 1859.

Migne, J. P., *Patrologiae Cursus Completus*—Series Latina, 221 vols., Paris, 1844-1855.

Roskovany, A., *De Matrimoniis Mixtis inter Catholicos et Protestantes*, Pestini, 1854.

Theodosiani Libri XVI cum Constitutionibus Sirmondianis, ed. Th. Mommsen, Berlin, 1905.

Authors

Adam, Karl, *The Spirit of Catholicism*, New York, 1931.

Albitius, Francis, *De Inconstantia in Iure Admittenda vel Non*, Amsterdam, 1683.

American Law Institute, *Restatement of the Law of Contracts*, 2 vols., St. Paul, 1932.

Aquinas, St. Thomas, *Summa Theologica.*

——, *Summa Contra Gentiles*, ed. I. Bertrand, Paris, 1878.

Augustine, Charles, *A Commentary on the New Code of Canon Law*, 8 vols., St. Louis, 1918-1922.

Ayrinhac, H. A.-Lydon, P. J., *Marriage Legislation in the New Code of Canon Law*, rev. ed., New York, 1932.

Bellarmine, Robert, *De Sacramentis Matrimonio*, Naples, 1872.

Blackstone, William, *Commentaries on the Laws of England*, 2 vols., Philadelphia, 1882.

Burns, J. A., *Catholic Education*, New York, 1917.

Cappello, Felix M., *Tractatus Canonico-Moralis de Sacramentis*, 3 vols., Turin, 1927.

Cardozo, Benjamin N., *The Growth of the Law*, New Haven, 1931.

——, *The Nature of the Judicial Process*, New Haven, 1928.

Chafee, Z., *Introduction to Pound's Cases on Equitable Relief against Defamation and Injuries to Personality*, 2nd ed., Cambridge, 1930.

——, "The Progress of the Law; Equitable Relief against Torts", in *Harvard Law Review*, 1921.

Corbett, Percy Elwood, *The Roman Law of Marriage*, Oxford, 1930.

De Becker, Julius, *De Sponsalibus et Matrimonio Praelectiones Canonicae*, 2nd ed., Louvain, 1903.

De Smet, A., *Tractatus Theologico-Canonicus de Sponsalibus et Matrimonio*, 4th ed., Bruges, 1927.

Esmein, A., *Le mariage en droit canonique*, 2 vols., Paris, 1891.

Feije, H. J., *Dissertatio Canonica de Matrimoniis Mixtis*, Louvain, 1847.

Frank, J., *Law and the Modern Mind*, New York, 1930.

Friedman, J., "The Parental Right to Control the Religious Education of the Child", in *Harvard Law Review*, 1916.

Funk, F. X., *History of the Church*, 2 vols., London, 1914.

Gasparri, P., *Tractatus Canonicus de Matrimonio*, 3rd ed., 2 vols., Paris, 1904.

——, *The Catholic Catechism*, New York, 1932.

Healy, P. J., *The Valerian Persecution*, Boston, 1905.

James, William, *The Varieties of Religious Experience*, New York, 1925.

Kelly, J. P., *The Jurisdiction of the Simple Confessor*, Washington, 1927.

Knecht, A., *Handbuch des Katholischen Eherechts*, Freiburg, 1928.

Köhne, J., *Die Ehen Zwischen Christen und Heiden in den Ersten Christlichen Jahrhunderten*, Paderborn, 1931.

Leo XIII, *Great Encyclical Letters*, New York, 1903.

Madden, Joseph W., *Handbook of the Law of Persons and Domestic Relations*, St. Paul, 1931.

Malloy, J. D., *A Catechism for Inquirers*, 4th ed., New York, 1927.

Motry, H. L., *Diocesan Faculties according to the Code of Canon Law*, Washington, 1922.

McCurdy, W. E., *Torts Between Persons in Domestic Relations*, in *Harvard Law Review*, 1930.

Nau, L. J., *Manual on the Marriage Laws of the Code of Canon Law*, New York, 1933.

O'Keeffe, G. M., *Matrimonial Dispensations; Powers of Bishops, Priests and Confessors*, Washington, 1927.

O'Neil, W. H., *Papal Rescripts of Favor*, Washington, 1930.

Payen, G., *De Matrimonio in Missionibus ac potissimum in Sinis*, Zi-Ka-Wei, 1929.

Peck, E., *Domestic Relations*, 3rd ed., Chicago, 1930.

Pesch, Tilmann, *The Christian Philosophy of Life*, London, 1909.

Petrovits, J. J. C., *New Church Law on Matrimony*, 2nd ed., Philadelphia, 1926.

Pius XI, *The Christian Education of Youth* (N. C. W. C. trans.), Washington, 1930.

Pomeroy, John N., *A Treatise on Equity Jurisprudence*, 3 vols., San Francisco, 1918-19.

Pound, Roscoe, "Interests of Personality", in *Harvard Law Review*, 1915.

——, "Individual Interests in Domestic Relations", in *Harvard Law Review*, 1916.

——, "Equitable Relief against Defamation and Injuries to Personality", in *Harvard Law Review*, 1916.

Prat, Fernand, *The Theology of St. Paul*, 2 vols., London, 1926.

Pratt, James Bissett, *The Religious Consciousness*, New York, 1920.

Rashdall, Hastings, *Philosophy and Religion*, New York, 1910.

Sangmeister, J. V., *Force and Fear*, Washington, 1932.

Schenk, F., *Mixed Religion and Disparity of Cult*, Washington, 1929.

Schouler, James, *A Treatise on the Law of Domestic Relations*, Albany, 1921.

Shahan, Thomas J., *The Beginnings of Christianity*, New York, 1903.

Sherman, C. P., *Roman Law in the Modern World*, Boston, 1917.

Spirago, F.–Clarke, R. F., *The Catechism Explained*, New York, 1927.

Starbuck, Edwin D., *The Psychology of Religion*, London, 1899.

Story, Joseph, *Commentaries on the Conflict of Laws, Foreign and Domestic, in Regard to Contracts, Rights, and Remedies, and especially in Regard to Marriages, Divorces, Wills, Successions and Judgments*, 8th ed., Boston, 1883.

Tanquerey, Adolphe, *The Spiritual Life*, Tournai, 1930.

——, *Synopsis Theologiae Moralis*, 3 vols., Paris, 1925.

Ter Haar, F., *De Matrimoniis Mixtis Eorumque Remediis*, Turin, 1931.

Ter Haar, F.–Connell, F. J., *Mixed Marriages and their Remedies*, New York, 1933.

Tiffany, Walter C., *Handbook on the Law of Persons and Domestic Relations*, 3rd ed., St. Paul, 1921.

Vermeersch, A.–Creusen, J., *Epitome Iuris Canonici*, 3 vols., Rome, 1928.

Vlaming, T. M., *Praelectiones Iuris Matrimonii*, 3rd ed., 2 vols., Bois de Duc, 1919.

Vromant, G., *Ius Missionarum* (Vol. V) *De Matrimonio*, Louvain, 1931.

Wambaugh, Eugene, *The Study of Cases*, 2nd ed., Boston, 1894.

Warren, Samuel D.–Brandeis, Louis D., "The Right of Privacy", in *Harvard Law Review*, 1890.

Wernz, F. X.–Vidal, P., *Ius Canonicum ad Codicis Normam Exactum*, 3 vols., Rome, 1927-1928.

Williston, Samuel, *The Law of Contracts*, 5 vols., New York, 1922-1927.

Wilmers, W., *Handbook of the Christian Religion*, 3rd ed., ed. James Conway, New York, 1901.

Woywod, S., *A Practical Commentary on the Code of Canon Law*, 2 vols., New York, 1925.

Periodicals

American Ecclesiastical Review, The, Philadelphia, 1889—
Apollinaris, Rome, 1928—
Bulletin of the International Federation of Catholic Alumnae, Washington, 1914—
Catholic Mind, The, New York, 1903—
Catholic World, The, New York, 1865—
Christian Century, The, Chicago, 1884—
Ephemerides Theologicae Lovanienses, Louvain, 1924—
Harvard Law Review, The, Cambridge, 1887—
Homiletic Review, The, New York, 1876—
Homiletic and Pastoral Review, The, New York, 1900—
Irish Ecclesiastical Record, The, Dublin, 1864—
Ius Pontificium, Rome, 1921—
Kentucky Law Journal, The, Frankfort, 1912—
Nouvelle Revue Theologique, Paris, 1868—
Yale Law Journal, The, New Haven, 1891—

BIOGRAPHICAL NOTE

Robert James White was born in 1893 in Concord, Massachusetts. He received his elementary and secondary education in Watertown, Mass. Pursuing further studies, he received the decree Bachelor of Arts from Harvard University in 1915. He entered Harvard Law School in the same year. The course was interrupted by two years service in the United States Navy during the World War. He received the degree Bachelor of Laws from Harvard Law School in 1920. He practiced law in Boston for eight years, serving part of the time as Assistant District Attorney for Middlesex County. He is a member of the Bars of the Supreme Judicial Court of Massachusetts, the United States District Court for Massachusetts, the United States Circuit Court of Appeals for the First Circuit, the Supreme Court of the District of Columbia and the United States Supreme Court. He entered the Sulpician Seminary in the Catholic University of America as a theological student and was ordained in 1931. He received the degree of Bachelor of Sacred Theology from the Catholic University of America in 1931.

APPENDIX

SUPREMA SACRA CONGREGATIO S. OFFICII.

Decretum de Cautionibus in Mixtis Nuptiis Praestandis

Contingit aliquando mixta, quae vocant, matrimonia inter catholicum et acatholicum sive baptizatum sive non baptizatum contrahi, praestitis quidem requisitis cautionibus, eo tamen modo ac forma ut earum observantia, praesertim quod spectat ad catholicam prolis utriusque sexus educationem, aliquibus in regionibus, adversantibus, legibus civilibus, efficaciter urgeri non possit, imo tum a locali auctoritate laica tum a ministro haeretico, invitis quoque parentibus, facile queat impediri.

Ne lex tam gravis, naturalis ac divini iuris, magno cum innocentium animarum detrimento, frustrata maneat, Emi ac Revmi Dni Cardinales fidei ac morum integritati tutandae praepositi, in plenario conventu habito feria IV die 13 Ianuarii 1932, prae oculis etiam habentes recentes, Ssmi Domini Nostri Encyclicas Litteras, quarum initium *Casti connubii,* stricti sui muneris esse duxerunt, omnium Sacrorum Antistitum nec non parochorum aliorumque, de quibus in canone 1044, qui super mixtae religionis ac disparis cultus impedimentis dispensandi facultate aucti sunt, attentionem excitare et conscientiam convenire, ne dispensationes huiusmodi unquam impertiantur, nisi praestitis antea a nupturientibus cautionibus, quarum fidelem exsecutionem, etiam vi legum civilium, quibus alteruter subjectus sit, vigentium in loco actualis vel (si forte alio discessurii praevideantur) futurae eorum commorationis, nemo praepedire valeat, secus ipsa dispensatio sit prorsus nulla et invalida.

Hanc vero Emorum Patrum resolutionem feria v die 14 eiusdem mensis et anni Ssmus D. N. Pius divinae Providentiae Pp. XI confirmavit et publici iuris fieri iussit, mandans ad quos spectat ut eam servent ac servarè faciant.

A. SUBRIZ, *Supr. S. Congr. S. Officii Notarius.*

L. * S.

CANON LAW STUDIES

1. Freriks, Rev. Celestine A., C.PP.S., J.C.D., Religious Congregations in Their External Relations, 121 pp., 1916.
2. Galliher, Rev. Daniel M., O.P., J.C.D., Canonical Elections, 117 pp., 1917.
3. Borkowski, Rev. Aurelius L., O.F.M., De Confraternitatibus Ecclesiasticis, 136 pp., 1918.
4. Castillo, Rev. Cayo, J.C.D., Disertacion Historico-canonica sobre la Potestad del Cabildo en Sede Vacante o Impedida del Vicario, Capitular, 99 pp., 1919 (1918).
5. Kubelbeck, Rev. William J., S.T.B., J.C.D., The Sacred Penitentiaria and Its Relations to Faculties of Ordinaries and Priests, 129 pp., 1918.
6. Petrovits, Rev. Joseph J. C., S.T.D., J.C.D., The New Church Law on Matrimony, X-461 pp., 1919.
7. Hickey, Rev. John J., S.T.B., J.C.D., Irregularities and Simple Impediments in the New Code of Canon Law, 100 pp., 1920.
8. Klekotka, Rev. Peter J., S.T.B., J.C.D., Diocesan Consultors, 179 pp., 1920
9. Wannenmacher, Rev. Francis, J.C.D., The Evidence in Ecclesiastical Procedure Affecting the Marriage Bond, 1920. (Not Printed.)
10. Golden, Rev. Henry Francis, J.C.D., Parochial Benefices in the New Code, IV-119 pp., 1921. (Printed 1925.)
11. Koudelka, Rev. Charles J., J.C.D., Pastors, Their Rights and Duties According to the New Code of Canon Law, 211 pp., 1921.
12. Melo, Rev. Antonius, O.F.M., J.C.D., De Exemptione Regularium, X-188 pp., 1921.
13. Schaaf, Rev. Valentine Theodore, O.F.M., S.T.B., J.C.D., The Cloister, X-180 pp., 1921.
14. Burke, Rev. Thomas Joseph, S.T.B., J.C.D., Competence in Ecclesiastical Tribunals, IV-117 pp., 1922.
15. Leech, Rev. George Leo, J.C.D., A Comparative Study of the Constitution "Apostolicae Sedis" and the "Codex Juris Canonici," 179 pp., 1922.
16. Motry, Rev. Hubert Louis, S.T.D., J.C.D., Diocesan Faculties according to the Code of Canon Law, II-167 pp., 1922.
17. Murphy, Rev. George Lawrence, J.C.D., Delinquencies and Penalties in the Administration and the Reception of the Sacraments, IV-121 pp., 1923.

18. O'REILLY, REV. JOHN ANTHONY, S.T.B., J.C.D., Ecclesiastical Sepulture in the New Code of Canon Law, II-129 pp., 1923.
19. MICHALICKA, REV. WENCESLAS CYRILL, O.S.B., J.C.D., Judicial Procedure in Dismissal of Clerical Exempt Religious, 107 pp., 1923.
20. DARGIN, REV. EDWARD VINCENT, S.T.B., J.C.D., Reserved Cases According to the Code of Canon Law, IV-103 pp., 1924.
21. GODFREY, REV. JOHN A., S.T.B., J.C.D., The Right of Patronage According to the Code of Canon Law, 153 pp., 1924.
22. HAGEDORN, REV. FRANCIS EDWARD, J.C.D., General Legislation on Indulgences, II-154 pp., 1924.
23. KING, REV. JAMES IGNATIUS, J.C.D., The Administration of the Sacraments to Dying Non-Catholics, V-141 pp., 1924.
24. WINSLOW, REV. FRANCIS JOSEPH, A.F.M., J.C.D., Vicars and Prefects Apostolic, IV-149 pp., 1924.
25. CORREA, REV. JOSE SERVELION, S.T.L., J.C.D., La Potestad Legislativa de la Iglesia Católica, IV-127 pp., 1925.
26. DUGAN, REV. HENRY FRANCIS, M.A., J.C.D., The Judiciary Department of the Diocesan Curia, 87 pp., 1925.
27. KELLER, REV. CHARLES FREDERICK, S.T.B., J.C.D., Mass Stipends, 167 pp., 1925.
28. PASCHANG, REV. JOHN LINUS, J.C.D., The Sacramentals According to the Code of Canon Law, 129 pp., 1925.
29. PIONTEK, REV. CYRILLUS, O.F.M., S.T.B., J.C.D., De Indulto Exclaustrationis necnon Saecularizationis, XIII-289 pp., 1925.
30. KEARNEY, REV. RICHARD JOSEPH, S.T.B., J.C.D., Sponsors at Baptism According to the Code of Canon Law, IV-127 pp., 1925.
31. BARTLETT, REV. CHESTER JOSEPH, A.M., LL.B., J.C.D., The Tenure of Parochial Property in the United States of America, V-108 pp., 1926.
32. KILKER, REV. ADRIAN JEROME, J.C.D., Extreme Unction, V-425 pp., 1926.
33. McCORMICK, REV. ROBERT EMMETT, J.C.D., Confessors of Religious, VIII-266 pp., 1926.
34. MILLER, REV. NEWTON THOMAS, J.C.D., Founded Masses According to the Code of Canon Law, VII-93 pp., 1926.
35. ROELKER, REV. EDWARD G., S.T.D., J.C.D., Principles of Privilege According to the Code of Canon Law, XI-166 pp., 1926.
36. BAKALARCZYK, REV. RICHARDUS, M.I.C., J.U.D., De Novitiatu, VIII-208 pp., 1927.
37. PIZZUTI, REV. LAWRENCE, O.F.M., J.U.L., De Parochis Religiosis, 1927. (Not Printed.)
38. BLILEY, REV. NICHOLAS MARTIN, O.S.B., J.C.D., Altars According to the Code of Canon Law, XIX-132 pp., 1927.
39. BROWN, BRENDAN FRANCIS, A.B., LL.M., J.U.D., The Canonical Juristic Personality with Special Reference to its Status in the United States of America, V-212, pp., 1927.

40. Cavanaugh, Rev. William Thomas, C.P., J.U.D., The Reservation of the Blessed Sacrament, VIII-101 pp., 1927.
41. Doheny, Rev. William J., C.S.C., A.B., J.U.D., Church Property: Modes of Acquisition, X-118 pp., 1927
42. Feldhaus, Rev. Aloysius H., C.PP.S., J.C.D., Oratories, IX-141 pp., 1927.
43. Kelly, Rev. James Patrick, A.B., J.C.D., The Jurisdiction of the Simple Confessor, X-208 pp., 1927.
44. Neuberger, Rev. Nicholas J., J.C.D., Canon 6 or the Relation of the Codex Juris Canonici to the Preceding Legislation, V-95 pp., 1927.
45. O'Keeffe, Rev. Gerald Michael, J.C.D., Matrimonial Dispensations, Powers of Bishops, Priests, and Confessors, VIII-232 pp., 1927.
46. Quigley, Rev. Joseph, A.M., A.B., J.C.D., Condemned Societies, 139 pp., 1927.
47. Zaplotnik, Rev. Ioannes Leo, J.C.D., De Vicariis Foraneis, X-142 pp., 1927.
48. Duskie, Rev. John Aloysius, A.B., J.C.D., The Canonical Status of the Orientals in the United States, VIII-196 pp., 1928.
49. Hyland, Rev. Francis Edward, J.C.D., Excommunication, Its Nature, Historical Development and Effects, VIII-181 pp., 1928.
50. Reinmann, Rev. Gerald Joseph, O.M.C., J.C.D., The Third Order Secular of Saint Francis, 201 pp., 1928.
51. Schenk, Rev. Francis J., J.C.D., The Matrimonial Impediments of Mixed Religion and Disparity of Cult, XVI-318 pp., 1929.
52. Coady, Rev. John Joseph, S.T.D., J.U.D., A.M., The Appointment of Pastors, VIII-150 pp., 1929.
53. Kay, Rev. Thomas Henry, J.C.D., Competence in Matrimonial Procedure, VIII-164 pp., 1929.
54. Turner, Rev. Sidney Joseph, C.P., J.U.D., The Vow of Poverty, XLIX-217 pp., 1929.
55. Kearney, Rev. Raymond A., A.B., S.T.D., J.C.D., The Principles of Delegation, VII-149 pp., 1929.
56. Conran, Rev. Edward James, A.B., J.C.D., The Interdict, V-163 pp., 1930.
57. O'Neil, Rev. William H., J.C.D., Papal Rescripts of Favor, VII-218 pp., 1930.
58. Bastnagel, Rev. Clement Vincent, J.U.D., The Appointment of Parochial Adjutants and Assistants, XV-257 pp., 1930.
59. Ferry, Rev. William A., A.B., J.C.D., Stole Fees, X-107 pp., 1930.
60. Costello, Rev. John Michael, A.B., J.C.D., Domicile and Quasi-Domicile, VII-201 pp., 1930.
61. Kremer, Rev. Michael Nicholas, A.B., S.T.B., J.C.D., Church Support in the United States, VI-136 pp., 1930.
62. Angulo, Rev. Luis, C.M., J.C.D., Legislación de la Iglesia sobre la intención en la aplicación de la Santa Misa, VII-104 pp., 1931.

63. Frey, Rev. Wolfgang Norbert, O.S.B., A.B., J.C.D., The Act of Religious Profession, VIII-174 pp., 1931.
64. Roberts, Rev. James Brendan, A.B., J.C.D., The Banns of Marriage, XIV-140 pp., 1931.
65. Ryder, Rev. Raymond Aloysius, A.B., J.C.D., Simony, IX-151 pp., 1931.
66. Campagna, Rev. Angelo, Ph.D., J.U.D., Il Vicario Generale del Vescovo, VII-205 pp., 1931.
67. Cox, Rev. Joseph Godfrey, A.B., J.C.D., The Administration of Seminaries, VI-124 pp., 1931.
68. Gregory, Rev. Donald J., J.U.D., The Pauline Privilege, XV-165 pp., 1931.
69. Donohue, Rev. John F., J.C.D., The Impediment of Crime, VIII-110 pp., 1931.
70. Dooley, Rev. Eugene A., O.M.A., J.C.D., Church Law on Sacred Relics, IX-143 pp., 1931.
71. Orth, Rev. Clement Raymond, O.M.C., J.C.D., The Approbation of Religious Institutes, 171 pp., 1931.
72. Pernicone, Rev. Joseph M., A.B., J.C.D., The Ecclesiastical Prohibition of Books, XII-267 pp., 1932.
73. Clinton, Rev. Connell, A.B., J.C.L., The Paschal Precept, 1932.
74. Donnelly, Rev. Francis B., A.M., S.T.L., J.C.L., The Diocesan Synod, 1932.
75. Torrente, Rev. Camilo, C.M.F., J.C.L., Las Processiones Sagradas, 1932.
76. Murphy, Rev. Edwin J., C.PP.S., J.C.L., Suspension Ex Informata Conscientia, 1932.
77. MacKenzie, Rev. Eric F., A.M., S.T.L., J.C.L., The Delict of Heresy in its Commission, Penalization, Absolution, 1932.
78. Lyons, Rev. Avitus E., S.T.B., J.C.L., The Collegiate Tribunal of First Instance, 1932.
79. Connolly, Rev. Thomas A., J.C.L., Appeals, 1932.
80. Sangmeister, Rev. Joseph V., A.B., J.C.L., Force and Fear as Precluding Matrimonial Consent, 1932.
81. Jaeger, Rev. Leo A., A.B., J.C.L., The Administration of Vacant and Quasi-Vacant Episcopal Sees in the United States, 1932.
82. Rimlinger, Rev. Herbert T., J.C.L., Error Invalidating Matrimonial Consent, 1932.
83. Barrett, Rev. John D. M., S.S., J.C.L., Comparative Study of the Third Plenary Council and the Code, 1932.
84. Carberry, Rev. John J., S.T.D., Ph.D., J.C.L., The Juridical Form of Marriage, 1934.
85. Dolan, Rev. John L., A.B., J.C.L., The Defensor Vinculi, 1934.
86. Hannan, Rev. Jerome D., A.M., S.T.D., LL.B., J.C.L., The Canon Law of Wills, 1934

87. LEMIEUX, REV. DELISLE A., A.M., J.C.L., The Sentence in Ecclesiastical Procedure, 1934.
88. O'ROURKE, REV. JAMES J., A.B., J.C.L., Parish Registers, 1934.
89. TIMLIN, REV. BARTHOLOMEW, O.F.M., A.M., J.C.L., Conditional Matrimonial Consent, 1934.
90. WAHL, REV. FRANCIS X., A.B., J.C.L., The Matrimonial Impediment of Consanguinity and Affinity, 1934.
91. WHITE, REV. ROBERT J., A.B., LL.B., S.T.B., J.C.L., The Canonical Ante-Nuptial Promises in the Civil Law, 1934.

www.ingramcontent.com/pod-product-compliance
Lightning Source LLC
LaVergne TN
LVHW050218080826
844660LV00012B/432

* 9 7 8 0 8 1 3 2 2 2 8 0 6 *